Immigrants In Their Own Voice

The Torch Still Burning Bright

Alexander Kugushev

Dedication

To my love, Mimi, who is also my wife, and who has opened me to all of life's possibilities.

Contents

Why this book? Why Now?

My erudite Russian grandfather had never been in America. During my European adolescence, he once told me that on a Wednesday afternoon the president of America would sit on the porch of the White House. One could walk up and talk to him. That was probably Andy Jackson, but this story remained with me, and early on I grew a strong affinity for America, the land of the free and the equal.

Though born in France and schooled successively in Yugoslavia, Switzerland, and Argentina, America never ceased to call me. In an exploratory mode I finally immigrated, ready to return to a well-paid job in Argentina if I found the United States disappointing. It took me two weeks to decide that I would become American. Though I didn't understand most of what surrounded me, I saw exhilarating freedom and openness.

As a citizen for many decades now, I have not wavered from my initial impression, despite understanding much and disliking some. But I have also come to worry that a majority of native-born Americans don't share my and most immigrants' faith in the United States.

It seems that we don't want any more immigrants—the builders of America. This is a timely matter. Will we cease to be a country of the future, retreating into a defensive shell? We need a new, well-thought-out immigration policy...now. It needs to stimulate lawful immigration that will continue to grow this country. I hope that this book can contribute to the debate.

❖ ❖ ❖

I have populated the following chapters with the voices of actual immigrants and of their children and grandchildren. Most I quote anonymously to allow their voices to speak spontaneously. I have kept the actual names of three interviewees, with their permissions: Lisceth Cruz, from Mexico; Linda Katehi, from Greece; and Jian Liu, from China. All three bring us the most valuable immigrant gift: the enhancement of our education. Cruz is completing her PhD dissertation in higher education. Katehi is the chancellor of the University of California, Davis, and a creative educational innovator. Liu brings extraordinary dedication to teaching mathematics to our high school students.

Acknowledgements

Doug Adams, Nancy Evans, Bea and Bob Gormley, and Alice Ralph have generously contributed to the development of this book through their intellectual insights and editorial advice. I owe them gratitude for strengthening the coherence and persuasiveness of my arguments. Any inadequacies of this book are, of course, entirely my responsibility.

1

Why We Need Immigrants

We want immigrants because they enrich the US. I want this country to prosper for my grandchildren.

—RICK, IMMIGRANT FROM IRAN

Are we forgetting who we are: a nation of immigrants who came with strong arms, determined minds, courageous hearts, optimism, hope, and dreams to build a country more free and prosperous than any?

As the country matured, successive generations have lost contact with the lives and memories of their immigrant ancestors. Having no personal experience of the pioneering spirit has led to a decrease in national confidence by too many Americans. Googling "American decline" provides dozens of lamentation sites. They declare the collapse of the American Dream, the dysfunction of the political system, the instability of the economy, degradation of morality, and assorted other reasons to despair for this country's future—a vision of the American glass half empty.

Such pessimism masks our great enduring strengths of constant regeneration and renewal. In its current predicaments, this resilient nation merely transits through another stage. But it needs booster shots.

Immigrants see the American glass half full. They can reenergize our engine…if we allow them. They drove our young nation onward and can do it again. We need their force and their spirit to reconnect us to our original optimism, convictions, and cultural vigor. In this book, their voices speak. They tell us how they can help us and why we need them.

Who Are They?

We fit many categories under the label "immigrant": those who come legally and those who don't; those driven by economic necessity and those escaping political persecution; those, and this includes me, who quest for freedom of self-expression. Some belong to sizeable groups, such as Chinese, Indians, and Mexicans. An infinite variety of others from across the globe belong to no large groupings. In 1890, the historic high, immigrants comprised about 14.8 percent of our population. Today they make up some 12.5 percent of it. About two-thirds of them dwell here legally as either naturalized citizens or as lawful permanent residents (more commonly known as "green card" holders). Of the approximately 10.8 million illegal immigrants, about 40 percent arrived legally but overstayed their visas.

Americans hold a range of expectations about immigrants. They want them to learn and speak English; to respect our culture and join us by becoming citizens; to contribute to our society and learn from it; to hold dear our Constitution; to act fairly and honestly and, of course, not break our laws; to work and be givers, not just takers; to be educated, or at least strive for education. In other words, we want them to practice what we consider our values.

Most legal immigrants successfully meet these expectations, some especially so. We currently perceive Chinese, Indians, Vietnamese, and Koreans as invariably educated and entrepreneurial and as parents who strive for their children to achieve the highest standards in education and otherwise.

Thomas Friedman and Michael Mandelbaum, in *That Used to Be Us*, understand well how we immigrants think: "It means approaching the world with the view that nothing is owed you, nothing is given, you have to make it on your own. There is no 'legacy' slot waiting for you at Harvard or the family firm or anywhere else. You have to go out and earn or create your place in the world. And you have to pay very close attention to the world you are living in."[1]

> For this book, I have interviewed persons from Argentina, Bulgaria, China, Colombia, Costa Rica, the Dominican Republic, El Salvador, England, Estonia, France, Germany, Greece, Hungary, India, Indonesia, Iran, Israel, Italy, Jamaica, Korea, Liberia, Malta, Mexico, Nicaragua, Pakistan, Philippines, Poland, Russia, Serbia, South Africa, Spain, Sweden, Syria, Taiwan, Turkey, Uganda, and Vietnam—a mere sampling of the infinite variety of immigrants to the United States.

What They Bring

For several indispensable reasons, we want immigrants.

To reaffirm our faith in America. As a national priority, we need to revive our collective spirit. This spirit comes naturally to most immigrants. In contrast to native-born doubters, most newcomers arrive bursting with energy, endowed with moderate optimism, proven courage, a desire to work, and an implicit faith in the promise of America. Generally youthful and positive, they invigorate and affirm our nation's spirit. This is their most valuable, if immeasurable and never mentioned contribution.

I have become a citizen because I found that I agree with the American system of beliefs and values. Also because of Americans' energy and willingness to change. No elites that pull up a ladder behind them in America. Upward flexibility allows one to rise to the limits of one's potential, and I find that I am free to develop myself fully in this country. Nor is America in decline. It continues to exhibit powerful streams of renewal and growth.

—*Will, South African immigrant, PhD physicist, married to an American*

To strengthen education. Too many native-born students drop out of high school or don't complete college. They avoid studying the harder stuff, the indispensable knowledge for the modern world: mathematics, engineering, and the sciences. In their aggregate, immigrants compensate for these educational deficiencies. Not all do, but those who do matter. Some come with hardly any schooling, but their children often graduate from college or better. Other immigrants achieve the ambitious educational aspirations with which they arrived. Highly educated immigrants enrich our educational system by teaching in it; others staff our most sophisticated science and technology endeavors.

Miguel came from Costa Rica at age fourteen, seeking an American high school education. He stayed on, earned a master's degree in electrical engineering from the University of California, worked for several companies, and eventually started his own. He became a citizen and has four children, all with advanced degrees.

To foster innovation and inventiveness. By typical newcomer temperament and often out of necessity, immigrants recognize opportunities to innovate and to invent. This renews our practices, institutions, and attitudes; challenges assumptions; and flushes out the superfluous, the dated, and the tired. Through their innovative impulses, immigrants strengthen our society's vigor and optimism.

The American environment encourages innovation. It is easy here to be stimulated to present new ideas. At company or professional meetings everybody tries to do their best and there is great openness to ideas. Innovation is also facilitated by easy access to open-minded venture capitalists. In France, where there are many people with brilliant ideas, innovation always needs to fit into a preexisting or preconceived condition.

—*Thierry, French electrical engineer with an American PhD, married to an American*

To spur economic vitality. Immigrants bring multiple benefits to the economy. All of them work, generally hard. They create new enterprises and expand employment. They assume risks as they optimistically invest. They contain inflation by working for modest wages. These wages allow some American jobs to remain stateside rather than moving overseas. Especially the educated and the highly skilled among them buttress our economy in the competitive global marketplace.

I immigrated, two months ago, with the express intention of starting a software company that would have a transformative effect. This I have done. Since my adolescence I had dreamed to study at MIT. Some years ago I realized that dream and earned an MBA at MIT. During that earlier stay in America, I observed much greater receptiveness to technological transformation than in any other country; also that the United States had the most favorable climate for such ventures, especially in California. I noticed an atmosphere of natural selection, which causes the best to come here, and was sure that we would find first-rate people to work with. Here I also found fantastic professional ethics. My company is international with headquarters in California and an office in Chile. We expect to be creating jobs in America.

—*Ariel, a young Argentine entrepreneur, married to a Costa Rican*

To energize and renew society. As they plant roots and become citizens, immigrants begin to deepen their influence on society, increasingly these days when so many more of them are educated. Their civic roles increase, and they vote and join community organizations. As they become more prosperous and influential, they and their descendants progressively join the elites of the nation. In the process they gradually replace some tired and dispirited elites of longer standing.

I am a citizen now and I vote, partly because I believe in the ideals upon which this country was founded, that all men are equal and have the same rights. Politically I am an independent, more likely a libertarian, by which I understand opposition to the idea of personal entitlement. This is a land where opportunity is achievable through one's work alone and everyone can go as far as their abilities can take them. I want to give my fellow citizens a sense of optimism about the future; that anything is possible here, but also that you can be happy with less than you think. To my children, I want to give an understanding of what they have and be grateful for it. Make them aware of the opportunities in America and that there is nothing to stop them.

—*Pascual, Dominican, computer programmer, married to an American*

To connect us to the world. The immigrants' children, the second generation, form a phalanx of exceptional influence. They are disproportionately well-educated and as a consequence often civically engaged. Their presence matters especially at the beginning of the twenty-first century, when they contribute a cosmopolitan outlook. The globe has integrated, and the United

States continues to play the dominant role. Yet too many native-born show no interest in other countries, let alone in world affairs, have never traveled abroad, and speak only one language—a luxury we can no longer afford.

I grew up in Chicago, but in both worlds—United States and El Salvador. Because I was exposed to two cultures, I think that I am different from other native-born. This is a big advantage. It makes me understand what it takes to be an American. As a result, I am more consciously patriotic in examining my country and assessing its faults and merits. My father escaped El Salvador's dictatorship and corruption. When I see elements of either in America I am particularly sensitive to them. It makes me able to question whether America lives up to the promise of its ideals. I am more wary of bad government and a better patriot for questioning authority.

—*Pablo, son of Salvadoran immigrants, lawyer, in the United States Foreign Service*

To counteract demographic decline. America's core population has stabilized at a level below natural replacement. A declining population grows older, hence less energetic, inventive, innovative, or committed to an optimistic future. Immigrants arrive overwhelmingly young, optimistic, and of childbearing age. Their overall fertility exceeds somewhat the rate needed for replacement (2.10 children per mother), which helps keep America's population at a stable replacement level. A youthful workforce also finances the retirement of an older population.

For all these reasons we should welcome a constant, intelligently managed stream of legal immigrants.

But Why Many Don't Want Them

PollingReport.com gauges public opinion systematically and frequently on immigration.[2] The responses oscillate, but they conclude on the whole that six out of ten Americans oppose new immigration—of any kind, legal or illegal, of the highly educated or the ignorant, even of those willing to work hard. Pertinent websites reveal that immigration opponents span a broad cross-section of opinion, from conservatives to liberals. Not only individuals oppose immigration, but entire organizations specialize in fighting it. The Federation for American Immigration Reform seeks a moratorium on immigration by anyone other than refugees and the spouses and minor children of US citizens. This moratorium would affect legal immigrants "until it can be shown that higher immigration levels are needed."[3]

Recent waves of illegal immigrants cause much consternation. But other factors also stir anti-immigrant emotions, prime among them the economic uncertainties and the rapid cultural changes of the modern world. Many fear competition for jobs at the lower level by illegal migrants and at the higher by well-educated foreigners. Others fret that the new arrivals will submerge the native Anglo-Saxon culture. John Tanton, eugenicist, wrote in 1993, "I've come to the point of view that for European-American society and culture to persist requires a European-American majority, and a clear one at that."[4] Overburdening the government, cost of health care, and increases in crime and terrorism also figure among the concerns.[5]

Some worry about the demographic and environmental consequences of more immigration. The site Progressives for Immigrant Reform (June 23, 2009) indicates that 67 percent of liberals and progressives feel that the level of population growth caused by immigration harms our quality of life, and 58 percent believe that the current levels of immigration damage the environment.

These concerns bear upon all immigrants, legal or illegal. Nor are they new. American nativism, older than the republic itself, adds impetus to current anti-immigration emotions. Malaria-like, nativism resides endemically in the national psyche and breaks out in periodic, fevered pitches. Different factors may trigger it. During times of economic insecurity, immigrants seem like threats to available employment and living wages (and currently to Social Security and Medicare).

At other times, when large numbers of non-Anglo-Saxon immigrants arrive, their linguistic, physical, and cultural differences appear as intolerable menaces to the established and highly successful (and ethnically superior) Anglo-Saxon model. The 9/11 event has added heightened suspicion of anyone not native-born. In response to hearing large numbers of recently added German accents in Pennsylvania in the 1740s, Benjamin Franklin wrote:

> Those who come hither are generally of the most ignorant Stupid Sort of their own Nation...and as few of the English understand the German Language, and so cannot address them either from the Press or Pulpit, 'tis almost impossible to remove any prejudices they once entertain...Not being used to Liberty, they know not how to make a modest use of it.

In the 1830s, Samuel Morse, artist and inventor, described immigrants as "outcast tenants of poorhouses and prisons of Europe, who would soon strangle a nation in its infancy."

In 1909, Senator Henry Cabot Lodge, Boston patrician, advocated administering literacy tests to "Italians, Russians, Poles, Hungarians, Greeks and Asiatics...In other words [races] with which the English-speaking people had never hitherto assimilated, and who are most alien to the great body of American people."[6]

Now at the beginning of the twenty-first century, nativism runs an especially acute fever, stimulated by particularly negative perceptions of "Hispanics." In 2000, famed Harvard professor Samuel Huntington opined, "Mexican immigration is a unique, disturbing, and looming challenge to our cultural integrity, our national identity, and potentially to our future as a country."

In 2009, Jay Severin, a radio talk show host, said about Mexicans: "It's millions of leeches from a primitive country come here to leech off you and, with it, they are ruining the schools, the hospitals, and a lot of life in America."[7]

All manifestations of nativism have one element in common: fear. Franklin, Cabot Lodge, and Huntington feared for the virtues of their homogenous culture. So did Morse, troubled by large numbers of new arrivals from unprecedented and disdained countries, especially of Catholics into then still very Protestant America. Severin's fears arise in a climate of enormous illegal immigration during a time of dire economic and employment conditions. The legal status of the immigrants doesn't appear to matter. Franklin, Morse, and Cabot Lodge inveighed against the legal kind, Huntington and Severin against the illegal. Each has perceived immigration in the context of his day, but the underlying throb of nativist apprehensions never dies.

Today's context, stimulated by anti-Hispanic feelings, is aggravated by Islamophobia—fear of Muslims in the wake of the 9/11 event and of subsequent terrorist threats from native-born and immigrant Muslims. Hostility toward these two groups metastasizes in much of public opinion into opposition to all immigration.

Whistling Dixie or Forging the Future

America cannot afford such untimely attitudes. As never before, the world challenges us to compete and to lead. This demands openness to the influx of fresh ideas, new energies, renewed work ethic, and full commitment to education. We cannot stagnate, looking backward and inward. About the roots of recent American overconfidence, Secretary of Education Arne Duncan said in 2010,

> It was a totally lethal combination of cockiness and complacency. We were the king of the world. But we lost our way. We rested on our

laurels…we kept telling ourselves all about what we did yesterday and living in the past. We have been slumbering and living off our reputation. We are like the forty-year-old who keeps talking about what a great high school football player he was.[8]

I advocate for legal immigration and believe that we should welcome any immigrants who meet our lawful criteria—including many worthy Muslims and Hispanics. Except for a few pertinent instances, illegal immigrants fall outside my scope.

In the following chapters, I aim to disprove, step by step, all the apprehensions and concerns uttered above, including financial and job loss fears and threats to our culture. I expect that the evidence in these chapters will demonstrate how uniformly and immensely beneficial immigrants are to America's vigorous progress.

We don't want immigrants?

2

Affirming Faith in America

~~

Immigrants who choose to stay lead the country by highlighting what's positive about the US. I believe that this is also my contribution.

—LINDA KATEHI, CHANCELLOR OF THE UNIVERSITY OF CALIFORNIA AT DAVIS, IMMIGRANT FROM GREECE

~~

The Immigrant Spirit

We miss immigrants' most important effect if we measure it solely in economic or material terms. Many native-born have come to doubt America. Such doubts hint at cracks in the nation's spirit. Most immigrants who stay and become naturalized trust that spirit.

I begin, therefore, this account of the benefits migrants bring to us with their spirit—their most fundamental contribution. It buttresses all their activities and this country has prospered on it since its colonial inception. As that spirit arrives in the mental knapsack of each new immigrant generation, it kindles our fire.

By staying and becoming citizens, most of us immigrants implicitly affirm our faith in America's essential virtues and our commitment to its civics. In this, we compensate, to a degree, for the despondency of many native-born. Two starkly contrasting views of America:

> There is no hope or justice in America anymore and the American dream is dead.
>
> —*Jim, a history professor at St. Vincent College, whom I met a few months after immigrating in 1960. The first comment of many in the same vein I heard over the following half century.*

> I came to fulfill myself and reach my potential. I found in America an open, expanding, accepting, accommodating society. People, rich and white, have been very supportive of me. There is every opportunity to move ahead, despite some confining, ambivalent attitudes toward blacks.
>
> —*Peter, Ugandan immigrant, age twenty-six, majoring in political science at the University of California, Berkeley. He hopes to go on to law school but not to become a lawyer.*

Peter expresses a common immigrant response to the welcoming openness of America. In turn he brings focused, optimistic discipline in contrast to the misapprehended pursuit of "happiness" proposed by some.

Mr. Adams and Mr. Powell

Waves of immigrants and their immediate descendants have shaped America for nearly four centuries. They generated an optimistic, energetic, ambitious, and, at times, recklessly daring society. But in a mature America, most Americans have no personal exposure to immigrant parents and grandparents. This has consequences, among them the rise of pessimism and a decrease of positive expectations about this now adult republic.

Throughout our history some Americans showed diminishing optimism while others continued to project vigor. It depends, in part, on their pedigree.

Already in the nineteenth century, two leading Americans, Henry Adams and John Wesley Powell, exemplified such diverging trends. Adams, the grandson and great-grandson of presidents, stood as an eminent, influential intellectual—though something of an effete snob, too. Powell, the son of humble English immigrants, pioneered the exploration of the Colorado River and of much of the West, founded the US Geological Survey, and energetically promoted science.

Historian Donald Worster writes about Adams: "even in his youth [he] could see in Washington, and indeed in America, only a spoiled dream and a bleak future." But Worster describes Powell as "every inch a man of hope, one who believed in the unlimited promise of America and…in the unlimited promise of human intelligence."[1] Different pedigrees, diverging visions of America. Adams, favored by a privileged life, evolved through four generations to hold views anchored to the past. In this, not much different from Franklin, Morse, or Cabot Lodge. Powell, free of expectations of an unaltered continuity, saw America quite differently.

So, whither this country today? Only a spoiled dream and a bleak future or hope and belief in its unlimited promise? While many American natives may express pessimism, immigrants and their immediate descendants still mostly share Powell's vision of this country.

Attitudes

Our attitudes will determine our future. Today we hear voices that echo both Adams and Powell. Some rooted natives, echoing Henry Adams:

> The middle class has disappeared. We have a highway to poverty and no roads coming out. I fear for [those] who have been kicked out of their homes, could be living on the streets, and don't know how to get another job. Many of the millions of jobs lost I don't think are coming back. I am really afraid for the majority of Americans today.
> —*Suze Orman, author, in a TV interview*

> Arrogant and misguided American policies have headed us for a series of catastrophes comparable to our disgrace and defeat in Vietnam of even to the sort of extinction that befell our former fellow "superpower," the Soviet Union. Such a fate is by now probably unavoidable.
> —*Chalmers Johnson, author, Nemesis: The Last Days of the American Republic, 2007*

> America is coming apart...we are on a path of national suicide.
> —*Patrick Buchanan, author, Day of Reckoning, 2009*

> The downward spiral of our culture and the exponential, even cult-like growth of forces that threaten our long-standing secular and humanistic values are causes for increasing alarm.
> —*Morris Berman, author, Dark Ages America: The Final Phase of Empire, 2007*

By contrast, immigrant voices echo John Wesley Powell:

> This is the land where opportunity is achievable through one's work alone. I feel free here to explore my limits. Everyone can go as far as

their abilities can take them. That is how you can prove your worth. I appreciate the peace and security we enjoy and the ideals upon which this country was founded. People here don't realize how good it is. Doing any kind of work is sufficient to provide for life's essentials. As for whether America is in decline, that is ridiculous, if you look at the big picture. Think about what America was like fifty or a hundred years ago, about the place of women, how much better it is today. If everyone thought positively, despite all the changes and turbulence of the moment, we would be okay.

—*Pascual, Dominican immigrant, computer programmer, arrived at age twenty-six, married an American, now a citizen*

What do I like about America? For one, I own a business. I couldn't have done it in Spain in the 1970s and perhaps not even now. For another, if I behave lawfully and pay my taxes, nothing will happen to me. I will be protected by laws, unlike, for example, in Mexico. Things here are clear, orderly, and predictable.

—*Rodrigo, middle-aged Spanish immigrant, small business owner, married to a Mexican immigrant*

Opportunity is the most positive aspect of American life. Here you can achieve anything.

—*Tina, twenty-year-old Indonesian female immigrant and college student (though presumably Muslim, in appearance and action a normal American undergraduate)*

Buying into Our Culture

We cannot evaluate our future in merely quantifiable and material terms. Instead, attitudes we cannot measure define and delimit our capacity to believe, to conceive, and to act. Which attitudes will prevail? On polling evidence, many rooted natives agree all too often with Henry Adams and the other pessimists quoted earlier. Immigrants and their immediate descendants I interviewed concur, almost unanimously, with John Wesley Powell.

As an immigrant and keenly interested observer, *I have learned to distrust pessimistic native rhetoric.* The great majority of Americans I have known over the past half century demonstrated through their actions, rather than through the occasional negative talk, trust in enduring spiritual convictions. They practice faith in our institutions and commitment to our laws. They believe in our fundamental morality, hard work, and responsibility, and they strive to improve themselves. To those convictions, the American character adds optimism in action and an itch to invent and to innovate (more in chapter 4). All of it too valuable, none dispensable. Many immigrants agree:

> The best way to predict your future is to create it.
> —*A Mexican gardener in Menlo Park, California, sporting these words, in English, on his T-shirt. Has he not already adopted the best American can-do spirit?*

I asked naturalized citizens about their thoughts upon becoming American:

> America has affected me greatly. It allowed me to become myself. Though a university graduate in the Soviet Union, my dream was to do work that involved beauty: clothes design and improving a woman's image. Here I fulfilled that dream by becoming a beautician, work that gives me great satisfaction and makes me feel professionally fulfilled. In America you are treated with dignity for the work you do well. So, I love America, the greatest country in the world, and my principal feeling for it is gratitude. It has also provided opportunities for my children, both of whom are college graduates.
> —*Irina, who left the totalitarian Soviet Union in 1981*

My Americanization was gradual, but I have become a very committed American. What I like about America is opportunity, which in Costa Rica is very modest. Also freedom, tolerance, and acceptance of the outsider. Living here has opened my mind to options and alternatives that would not have occurred to me in Costa Rica. There we are taught the value of education so that we can get a good job. I got a good education in the US and a good job at a very large high-tech company. I felt unhappy and switched to a couple of start-ups in Silicon Valley. This led me to think that why should I not start a company? American ambient culture encourages innovation. Here failure is not feared. If you fail, it's a badge of honor; in Latin America it is a stigma.

—*Miguel, electrical engineer and entrepreneur, came from Coast Rica as a teenager to get an American education*

In America I have found tolerance, social and legal equality, and fairness. I have never experienced prejudice for religious reasons or any others, even though I am a Muslim.

—*Ahmed, Pakistani immigrant, engineer*

America provides a freedom to do and an environment that stimulates innovative thinking. It has allowed me to act to my full potential and develop every aspect of my interests. In Sweden I would always be scared that I might be infringing some customs or expectations. Nothing stopped me here. I came as an MD intern/researcher to the University of Oklahoma but gradually grew to wanting to become American and hence became an immigrant. The American Constitution inspired me. I trust it because it allows for constant change, which will not permit the US to decline. The preeminence of the law protects all. In Sweden the majority rules and the Supreme Court would side with the majority for that reason, even if the law should favor the minority.

—*Lennart, Swedish MD who came young and grew to become American*

Living in America has definitely affected me. It made me more receptive to everybody and to everything. I arrived open-minded about what I saw, and this has furthered my career. I found here freedom to do what I like. There is opportunity, if one is willing to work and has the knowledge. Also one can make mistakes and recover—America is a land of second chances, which wouldn't happen in Italy. I like it here, am comfortable, and have become an American citizen (but still miss my Italian family).

—*Silvana, came from Italy with a degree in economics, now an executive at a high-tech company*

As an immigrant myself, I found freedom, not of the political kind but at a deeper, personal level. American civilization harbors virtues of tolerance, of openness to change, and to the new and different. In this cultural climate, I discovered that nothing stood in the way of my becoming anything I was capable of.

Hard to convey such feelings to those who have not functioned in societies that constrain one's potential. There, history, culture, economics, or class structure circumscribe one's biography. Here, I have developed my biography unhindered. My belief in the value of the essentially English culture I found in America has caused me to think of myself as an honorary Anglo-Saxon of sorts. Enthusiastic American? Yes, like so many immigrants.

At this stage of mature America's development, we stand at a crossroads: coasting along or growing through meritocracy. Immigrants represent effort and, ultimately, meritocracy.

Delfina

Delfina was born in Nicaragua. She married at age seventeen and had her first daughter at nineteen. At that time, the Marxist Sandinista regime came to power in Nicaragua, installed a police state with political spies, and created economic conditions that impoverished the population. Life became unbearable for her and her husband. In 1984 they decided to emigrate, but they couldn't obtain visas from the United States consulate. They could, however, obtain Mexican visas as a transition to the United States.

In the meantime, Delfina's second daughter was born. As she was only a few months old, it would have been impossible to travel with her. They temporarily left her with relatives. Delfina, now twenty-three, her husband, his younger brother (aged sixteen), and her older daughter (now aged three) got underway. They collected all their savings and purchased airline tickets to Mexico. From Mexico City, they needed to reach Tijuana. There, Delfina's mother, who had already emigrated to the United States, had arranged for a coyote (smuggler of illegal immigrants) to bring them over the border to San Diego.

After landing in Mexico, they didn't have enough money to purchase airline tickets to Tijuana. They took a bus for a journey that lasted forty-eight hours. Mexican immigration officials stopped the bus periodically. Delfina and her family wouldn't talk because their Nicaraguan accents would betray them. Nonetheless, at one stop an immigration official singled out Delfina's husband and brother-in-law and required them to follow him into the immigration office. After half an hour, they hadn't returned, and the bus driver wanted to resume driving, but Delfina asked him for ten more minutes. She took her daughter and her purse and went to force the issue. The official would not give her a straight answer, but he was clearly fishing for a bribe. Delfina gave him her last $40, at which point he released her two men.

They finally reached Tijuana, where the coyote had already assembled a number of other people in a safe house. There they all remained for about a week. On one late afternoon, they began to walk in casual groups of two or three in the direction of the US border. After dark, they gathered again and trekked through open, uninhabited country. At one point they had to ascend what seemed to be a very steep mountain. On the way up, Delfina slipped, fell, and rolled several feet down the slope, injuring her leg. No one but her husband stopped to help her. The others just kept moving. Through all that her husband was carrying the three-year-old girl.

At length they arrived at the US border, which in and of itself presented no obstacle, but on the American side there were several houses, and the dogs began to bark. The people living there knew what was going on and didn't come out. Delfina and her party crossed that section and came upon a steel fence, into which the coyote had cut a camouflaged hole. It was just large enough to crawl through, but it exited onto a freeway. Fortunately, it was 2 a.m. and there was little traffic. They dashed across the freeway. On the other side, the coyote had a hidden car, into which fourteen of them piled like sardines. They had walked for ten hours. Forty-five minutes later they arrived in San Diego and went to another safe house. From there, Delfina phoned her mother in San Francisco and life in America began.

They moved to the San Francisco Bay Area. None of them knew English (Delfina now speaks excellent, though accented English). Her husband found a job at a gas station. She began to make tamales and sold them in the neighborhood. New acquaintances directed her to an Iranian who had a shirt factory. He hired her at a minimum wage of $3.50/hour and required her to iron and pin one hundred and sixty shirts in eight hours. He told her that he would fire her if she couldn't fulfill that quota. Delfina found it very hard but met his conditions and kept the job.

Meanwhile, she bought a dictionary and began to teach herself English. She established a goal to learn one new word every day. All the while she continued to make tamales and sold them in the evenings. Initially, adaptation to America was not always simple—even traffic lights seemed intimidating after small-town Nicaragua. Through further contacts, she found a job in the kitchen at San Francisco State University. They made her a cashier immediately even though she still knew little English. In the summer, when the university closed, she worked in a similar capacity at the Oakland Coliseum. During this time Delfina enrolled in night classes at City College of San Francisco to learn more English while still working full-time. (Twenty-five years later, she continues to take college classes to improve her English grammar.)

Another new friend worked for a wealthy household in a rich suburb of San Francisco. On one occasion, the owners hosted a large dinner party and her friend asked Delfina if she would help. Delfina gladly agreed. One of the guests, apparently taken by Delfina's work and attitude, called her the next day and offered her a job at a Palo Alto café she owned. Delfina found the job very tough but decided that in a year she would become the café's manager. It took her longer, but she has managed it now for over seventeen years.

She and her husband saved as much as they could. Once they had accumulated $10,000, they had a down payment to buy a house. In her coffee shop management job, Delfina was now making a munificent $3,500 a month. Soon they had saved an additional $40,000, and now she desired to live in a better house. She hired a crew of construction workers, expanded the house, beautified its yard, and installed marble counters in her kitchen and wooden panel walls in the living room.

Crucially, during all those years, she brought up three daughters. The third was born in the United States. All three have now graduated from college, the first two with advanced degrees. All three work professionally. Two are married to "Americans" and have four children between them. The third, still single and twenty-four, has a degree in business, manages a bank branch, and work on an MBA. She thinks of getting married at thirty, after having built a career, but she wonders where she'll find a good man. Delfina doesn't worry: "We know how to handle men."

I engaged Delfina in a dialogue:

What were your expectations about America?

I thought that America was rich and free and I dreamed that we could start a better life here. We were sure that we would have better opportunities than in Nicaragua and that we would be successful.

Do you have any regrets about immigrating?

No, of course not. All my dreams have been totally fulfilled. How could I be disappointed? For my fiftieth birthday, my husband surprised me and took me for a vacation to Europe—and we have a Mercedes.

In what ways has the immigration experience changed or affected you?

Living in America has improved me. I am better educated and more confident. I became an American to the point that I don't want to return to Nicaragua, even though we have some property there and could live comfortably on American retirement. My home is here now; my three daughters live here and so do my grandchildren.

What do you like about America?

Freedom of speech and the people, who are generous and helpful. I have never experienced racism or discrimination personally, though both exist throughout American society.

What don't you like about America?

How Americans are changing. They are no longer the generous people we met when we first came. The new generation is greedy and self-centered. The kids today have no parents.

How were your children affected by being daughters of immigrants?

They were greatly influenced by it. We raised them as Americans, but I think that they are different. We brought them up strictly and taught them our values: morality, compassion, that you don't deserve anything, that you work hard and that you must earn everything. I think that they practice these lessons. They are responsible and hard-working and don't assume that they are entitled to anything.

By immigrating have you taken any native's job?

No, of course not. No natives would have taken the jobs I did for as little as I was paid.

Is America in decline?

Yes, because the family is disintegrating and the social bonds are falling apart. I have read about Rome's decline and its families, too, disintegrated.

Affirming America

What's wrong with Delfina's story? Only that we don't have enough Delfinas. Of course, she committed an initial wrong by coming here illegally, though, to her credit, she tried the legal route. She more than redeemed herself through her exemplary hard work and steady will, through her persistent self-improvement, through having legalized her condition and becoming an American citizen. Most importantly, she brought up three exemplary and well-educated young American women imbued with a model ethic. Despite all the difficulties, she has held together a strong and productive family, paid her taxes, and never burdened American health and social services.

Uncommon Delfinas do not cause me to waver in my opposition to unlawful immigration, but I also wonder how many illegal Delfinas may have landed on immigrant wings to pollinate us. Listen to their voices—Delfina's, Chancellor Katehi's, or those of the other immigrants I quote above. They restate faith in America's continuity. Collectively, they speak to those spiritual qualities that distinguish the best of the American character. Their disciplined, optimistic, invigorating spirit cheerfully denies claims of America's decline.

We don't want immigrants?

3

Strengthening Education

～

- What mark do you expect to leave on America?
- Through my teaching. I am passionate about education. I hope to
share my immigrant experience with my students to inspire them.
Perhaps also my cultural background allows me to be more logical
in my explanations to the students.

—JIAN, YOUNG IMMIGRANT FROM CHINA

～

My account of the benefits immigrants bring to us began with their spirit, the foundation stone. I follow with education because all aspects of America's place in the in twenty-first century hinge on it.

While our educational system contains islands of excellence, some as good as the best in the world, a sea of mediocrity unfortunately surrounds them. In a global environment driven by science and technology, a society that lags in rigorous education dooms itself to stagnation followed by decline. Our economy, in particular, now depends on a drastic improvement in the education of the totality of our citizens. Yet the United States suffers from too many ruptures between modern educational needs and the academic performance of large segments of the core population.

Social and cultural reasons combine to hold us back. The precariousness of many poor and unstable black and other minority families hinders their children from achieving the needed scholastic levels. Many Hispanic families bring no tradition of commitment to education in addition to their poverty. More generally among the core native population, we see communities prouder of their high school football teams than of the number of seniors going on to college.

College graduation rates reflect a feeble socio-cultural commitment to education. The overall US college graduation rate in 2010 scored a not-too-glorious 62.6 percent, lowered in part by Hispanics and blacks (41.5 and 40.5 percent, respectively).[1] New York Times columnist Bob Herbert discusses with alarm the reasons why the United States has fallen in the percentage of young people with college degrees from first to twelfth among thirty-six developed nations. He concludes, "All that's at stake is our future."[2]

Among those graduating, some 83 percent choose majors in intellectually easier fields and shun the sciences, mathematics, or engineering.[3] Public figures proclaim, without much embarrassment, their ignorance of science and a mild disdain for knowledge.

In 2011, the SAT tests (assessing high school students' aptitude to do well in college) hit historical lows in reading and in writing. To a large extent, these lows resulted from a rapid increase in numbers of students taking SAT tests—specifically, by minorities that heretofore had not aspired to a college education. Our national interest demands that we integrate such students into our mainstream. This process, however, will take time.

But education-avid immigrants to the rescue. To a striking extent, many immigrants' lives and careers center on education. This benefits us in multiple ways:

- They teach and they learn.
- They take a direct role in improving our elementary and secondary education.
- They staff our colleges and universities, instructing hard subjects in which we graduate all too few potential native-born faculty.
- To a high degree, they enter science fields and engineering, where they earn a preponderance of doctorate degrees.
- Many, themselves often poor and uneducated, incite their children, America's future, to achieve higher education at a greater ratio than the native-born.
- Almost 50 percent of Asians graduate from college, mostly children and grandchildren of immigrants (while only 31 percent of "whites" do).[4]

Some immigrants, of course, remain indifferent to personal improvement, or to that of their children.

They Take Direct Action

For some immigrants, elementary and secondary education forms the purpose of their American lives. Norma Rodriguez, Jian Liu, and Lisceth Cruz illustrate direct immigrant contributions to American education.

Norma Rodriguez

The *San Francisco Chronicle* (June 6, 2010) describes the California Legislature's failure to enact school reform because of resistance by teachers' unions. But it also speaks about reform coming from below.

One school principal, Norma Rodriguez, an immigrant from Mexico, has implanted reform at Anthony Dorsa Elementary School in San Jose. At her school, 93 percent of students are Latino and 64 percent learn English. Norma has recruited parent volunteers, also mostly immigrants, to participate on campus in the education of their children. During the six years of Norma's tenure, the school's API scores have risen 138 points (an outstanding performance). In 2010, the National Association of Elementary School Principals named her national distinguished principal of the year. Of herself, Norma says that she arrived in the United States at age fourteen, dropped out of high school at sixteen, and had children at a very young age. She says that "a principal of one of my kids' schools encouraged me to get involved, even though I didn't speak the language. This made me who I am today...I knew I had to bring that to my parents." An educational leader rising from the ranks of immigrants.

PISA, the Programme for International Student Assessment, reports that in 2009 American secondary students ranked thirty-first in the world in mathematics, with a score of 487. Singapore, Hong Kong, Korea, and Finland scored 562, 555, 546, and 541, respectively—all small and ethnically and culturally homogeneous. Still, a pretty ugly American ranking in a world economy driven by science and technology. But consider Jian Liu.

Jian Liu

Jian arrived in New York in 2005 at age eighteen with only basic knowledge of English. He had just graduated from secondary school in Beijing, and his family decided to emigrate to America to give him a good education. He enrolled at the City College of New York (CCNY) and was accepted at the Teacher Academy, a prestigious scholarship program of the NYC Partnership for Teacher Excellence. There he studied mathematics with the explicit goal of becoming a mathematics teacher. In spring 2011, he graduated with a BA in pure mathematics, with minors in secondary math education and physics. While at CCNY, he also took a summer program of advanced courses at Columbia University.

It gets better. In spring 2011, he received a fellowship worth $100,000 from Math for America. This nonprofit organization aims to improve mathematics education in our public secondary schools. It recruits, trains, and retains outstanding mathematics teachers in a highly selective five-year program for talented students who commit to teach math in public schools. Jian is now an American citizen.

Or Lisceth Cruz, a young woman from Mexico whose goals embrace college education for all:

Lisceth Cruz

I arrived in America, with my parents, at age fifteen. My parents wanted to give me a good education and enrolled me in a good public high school. In my class I was the only Mexican, the only "non-white." It was uncomfortable at times; I felt discriminated against, and some teachers told me that I would never graduate or go to college because girls like me were expected to become pregnant before then. But I persisted and ignored the negative, determined to go on to college. A good counselor and a good teacher saw my potential and mentored me.

My grades were good enough that I was admitted to the [elite] University of California. There, too, I encountered mentors who nurtured my academic progress. While in high school, I had wanted to become a marine biologist, but as I matured, I decided to devote my life to education. My aim is to provide the conditions for all children to go to college, no matter how disadvantaged culturally or economically. I am now completing a PhD in higher education policy. I also volunteer by conducting workshops for low-educated Latino parents, to encourage them to send their children to college. When I tell them, in Spanish, that I almost have a doctorate degree, they gasp in disbelief, "A Latina with a doctorate degree!?" I hope to inspire them for their children's sake.

They Come to Study

The National Association of Foreign Students Advisors reports that, in 2008, 623,000 foreign students, a record number, studied on American campuses. The association estimated that they and their dependents also contributed $15.5 billion to the American economy.[5] This represented a significant direct financial boost to our higher education. Many of these students stay on and enhance our society in manifold ways. Jian Liu certainly epitomizes the immigrant who comes to study here and stays to benefit our country. Consider also:

Ahmed came from Pakistan to study for an engineering degree and then go home. But love (he married a Mexican immigrant) and America's tolerance, social and legal equality, and a fair chance to do anything you want enticed him to stay. He became a citizen, and contributes engineering knowledge to our economy.

Lennart, the young Swedish MD, came to do an internship at the Medical School at the University of Oklahoma. The university encouraged him to engage in medical research, and he made important discoveries. In the process he got to like American life, which allowed him to develop his career and fulfill himself better than he could in Sweden. He obtained a green card and then became a citizen.

Muhammad came from Iran to obtain an air conditioning engineering degree, which he did. He liked America, stayed, became a permanent resident and in his mind an immigrant, then a citizen. He worked very hard and started two companies.

Ghassan came from Syria to study engineering for a year, but met love, married, and stayed. He became an immigrant, then a citizen, and eventually earned a master's degree in engineering at Stanford University. He credits America for opportunities, choices, and the freedom to develop himself. Now he directs the civil engineering works of a major California city.

Anand came from India to study for an advanced degree in architecture, and planned to return to India to practice. But America seduced him. He found that opportunities were open to all, that the culture allowed one to become fully "me." He also liked that no religious preconceptions existed because business considerations trump religious ones, contrary to what happens in India. He stayed, founded an architectural firm, and became a citizen.

Linda came from Greece to study for an advanced degree in electrical engineering, not planning to stay in the United States. But as she worked toward a PhD, she gradually developed an understanding of and a strong faith in America. She became an immigrant and then citizen. She credits many reasons for her evolution, among them how women are treated here and the opportunities and support available to them (she says that women are not taken seriously in Greece). She came to believe in American social values, in how Americans respect work, in meritocracy above all.

We saw, of course, *Ariel* in the first chapter, who dreamed of study-ing some day at M.I.T. and realized his dream. He then came back, now as an immigrant, to found a software company in California.

To amplify this anecdotal evidence, 52 percent of immigrant founders of engineering and technology companies in the United States report that education was their original reason for coming to this country.[6] They came to study, but America lured them in and they reinvested their education in the United States.

They Educate Their Children

All my interviewees, educated or not, make the education of their children a paramount priority. The children of virtually every educated immigrant I interviewed have gone to college.

The son of the *Sikorskis*, immigrants from Poland, is working on a PhD in finance.

Edwin, the son of educated Jamaican immigrants, has graduated from Cornell and now pursues a graduate degree at the University of California, Berkeley.

Lennart, the medical doctor from Sweden, has a lawyer son and a financial executive daughter.

Zoia, a Russian immigrant, has a son, a lawyer and judge in Alaska and an artist daughter. Both followed postgraduate studies in Europe.

Vera, another Russian immigrant, pianist, and music teacher, has a daughter. Vera comments, "I tried to bring up my daughter to be an honorable, responsible, constructive member of society." She seems to have succeeded because her daughter has graduated with honors from the University of California, Berkeley, and now studies medicine.

In 2011, the book *Tiger Mom* by Amy Chua made waves. It recounts the Chinese-American author's obsessive perfectionism in the educational demands she placed on her daughters. My interviewee, highly educated *Meiying*, though not obsessed, well-represents Chinese immigrants' attitude toward education:

> In bringing up my two American children, I place my principal emphasis on education. This is especially hard to achieve in America, where education is on the whole very weak, because it teaches rote and not thinking and because it receives no support from the family. I teach them not to be competitive against others but to have high expectations of themselves in order to reach their full potential. Of course, I expect them both to go to college.

But it's not only the educated immigrants' children. Parents with only a grade school education also aspire to a college education for their children:

> *Delfina*, of course. Her three daughters have not only completed their college education, but have also obtained graduate degrees (the third is still pursuing an MBA, while also working full-time).

> *Esmeralda*, who received only a grade school education in Mexico, has two sons who graduated from college and a third still in high school.

> *Mercedes*, who also received a grade school education in Mexico, has two of her children in college, with two more to go.

> *Jane*, daughter of a fourth grade-educated mother from Mexico, graduated in 2011 from the University of California, Berkeley, with a major in sociology. She says, "Observing how my single mother acted as an immigrant has caused me to be determined and decide that I will not consider any doors closed. UC is an example where I am very much at ease."

Rodrigo completed his grade school education in Spain, and he is now the owner of a gardening service and is married to a Mexican immigrant. He has two teenage daughters: the older wants to study medicine, the younger to become a veterinarian. College bound!

Indian immigrants famously strive for high educational achievement for their children. This drive often manifests in the exceptional success of those children at the Scripps National Spelling Bee. Nine of the thirteen winners between 1999 and 2011 were children of Indian immigrants (in 2005, the top four finishers were). Balu Natarajan, the 1985 winner and now a doctor of sports medicine, says that the Indian record on spelling bees "gives the community quite a bit of confidence that we can do well here, much like other ethnicities pursuing the American dream."[7]

I have probably interviewed an uncommon sample because nationwide immigrant parents' commitment to education varies greatly. It depends, more often than not, on the extent of their education.

In *Exceptional Outcomes*, Patricia Fernandez-Kelly and Alejandro Portes study immigrants' children who have overcome especially dire handicaps in order to graduate from high school. Many among them have gone on to successful college studies. Without exception, their parents lacked education beyond grade school. The book reports, however, that academic success often depends on the family's cultural and national background. Thus, high school graduation rates varied in 2009: East Asians 72 percent, South East Asians 51 percent, Africans/Caribbeans 45 percent, Europeans 40 percent, Latin Americans 31 percent, but Mexicans only 15 percent.[8] These data apply overwhelmingly to second- and third-generation descendants of immigrants. By comparison, the overall US high school graduation rate that year stood at a frighteningly low 53 percent, burdened by high drop-out rates of core population students and of descendants of certain recent immigrant groups.

Despite some discouraging data reported by *Exceptional Outcomes*, strong educational progress occurs across generations. The children and grandchildren of immigrants in California and the nation as a whole tend to be much better educated than their parents. Among first-generation immigrants age fifty-seven to sixty-six, 36 percent have not graduated from high school. In the second generation, only 8 percent in the age cohort thirty to thirty-nine have failed to do so. After the second generation, the proportion of Californians age thirty to thirty-nine without high school diplomas drops to 6 percent.[9]

The cumulative effect of this intense commitment to education by immigrant parents has telling consequences. Economist David Card finds that "Second-generation sons and daughters [of immigrants] have higher education and wages than the children of natives. Even children of the least-educated immigrant origin groups have closed most of the education gap with the children of natives."[10]

They Staff Our Higher Education

We don't produce nearly enough scholars from native stock in fields that require rigorous, mathematical, and scientific thinking. In 2006, the National Science Foundation reported that only 15 percent of US college students earn degrees in the sciences and engineering. To staff our colleges and universities, we import scholars. A random examination of faculty rosters in engineering, mathematics, and statistics at several universities yields these results.

School	Department	Faculty	Foreign-born	National Origins
Pennsylvania State University	Mathematics	61	59%	Bulgaria, China, Russia, Senegal, U.K., Israel, Armenia, Rumania, Italy, Norway, Canada
Oklahoma State University	Electrical engineering	25	44%	Iran, India, and China
Mankato State University	Mathematics and statistics	16	56%	Korea, Russia, India and China
Rutgers State University	Electrical engineering	34	56%	Germany, Rumania, Serbia, Croatia, Bosnia, India, China, Greece, Italy, and Egypt
University of South Alabama	Mathematics and statistics	26	42%	Hungary, Germany, U.K., Russia, India, and China

At superlative MIT, foreign-born constitute more than 40 percent of the faculty in the School of Engineering.[11] At the University of California, Davis, some 35 percent of the faculty in the sciences and engineering are foreign-born and mostly immigrants. Chancellor Katehi says that this has a beneficial side effect by making the native-born faculty more cosmopolitan and world-conscious, all of which imbues the university's climate with modern world awareness. Very nice, of course, but the worrisome fact remains that without these foreign-born professors—not all necessarily immigrants—we couldn'tstaff the engines of our prosperity.

They Boost Science and Engineering

The preceding section highlights the inadequate commitment of the native-born to the study of the harder academic disciplines. The National Science Foundation reports that of the bachelor's degrees awarded in 1998, only 17.1 percent were in the sciences and engineering[12]:

- Physical sciences 1.3 percent
- Earth atmospheric and ocean sciences 0.4 percent
- Biological and agricultural sciences 7.1 percent
- Mathematics 1.0 percent!!
- Computer science 2.3 percent
- Engineering a paltry 5 percent

As we saw above, in 2006 even fewer earned degrees in the sciences and engineering. In 2008, one in four American workers with a degree in the sciences and engineering was over fifty years old. Aerospace giant Lockheed Martin plans to hire 142,000 engineers between 2011 and 2019, yet in 2011 only some sixty thousand engineers graduated from American universities to supply the needs of our entire economy.[13] Famed astronomer Carl Sagan wrote:

> We've arranged a global civilization in which most crucial elements profoundly depend on science and technology. We have also arranged things so that almost no one understands science and technology. This is a prescription for disaster. We might get away with it for a while, but sooner or later this combustible mixture of ignorance and power is going to blow up in our faces.

In this, too, immigrants aid us. The 2000 Census reported that while immigrants constitute 12.5 percent of the US population, almost half of scientists and engineers with doctorate degrees in the United States were immigrants. Nearly 70 percent of men and women who entered fields of science and engineering in the United States from 1994 to 2000 were immigrants, corroborating the Census findings.[14] We see in chapter 5, "Spurring the Economy," how this immigrant commitment to science and engineering benefits our economy.

Fallacies...

Alarmed voices denounce graduate-level education of foreigners because they "steal" American knowledge and then return to their countries and compete against us with what we invested in them. Typical examples of these concerns appear in an article by Tom Elias (July 15, 2011)[15]

> Says one prominent researcher at the UCLA medical school who has supervised MD and PhD holders from a variety of countries, "My main worry is over the 40 percent to 50 percent who go back to their home countries...They steal our way of thinking because there is little tradition of creative thinking in their own countries. There's a real rip-off occurring...The Chinese, for example, have no real higher educational system of their own, so they send people here to learn not only methods but also our ways of thinking. If even 40 percent return home, it's a terrific investment for them because now they have people who can start biotech and electronic companies without having to educate them themselves. Sometimes I think they are way too wily for us, and we're way too naïve to realize that we are being unpatriotic when we accept these guys.

From a Stanford University scientist, we hear, "I have had a technician in my lab for almost twenty years who leads a double life as a full professor in China, going back there four times a year for two or three weeks at a crack. He's training them in our methods and ways of thinking so they can compete with us." Such worries border on the silly. They ignore that:

- Foreign students pay for their education, thus richly supporting our universities.
- Sixty percent of them stay in the United States, becoming immigrants and eventually US citizens, as my interviews quoted above confirm.
- They invent, innovate, and start enterprises (see above and chapters 4, "Nurturing Innovation and Inventiveness" and 5, "Spurring the Economy").
- They teach scientific and technical subjects at our universities, matters in which we produce too few native scholars and researchers.
- If they return to their home countries, not necessarily for good, they spread American ideas and cultural influence. Such aspects of our soft power may mitigate autocratic politics and corrupt economics in some of those countries.

These complaints also ignore that all too many foreign students are forced to leave the United States upon completing their degrees because their visas expire. Tina's Indonesian parents brought her to America as a teenager so that she could obtain a good education. She has graduated with honors in mathematics and economics from the University of California Berkeley, and now pursues a PhD. She likes America because "it opened perspectives that I wouldn't have had in Indonesia and because there is opportunity; here you can achieve anything." She disapproves of other elements, however:

The stupid immigration policies. I have trouble getting permanent resident status and I want to become American. Even though the chancellor of the University of California has recommended me, apparently that doesn't faze the bureaucrats.

There will be more on such self-defeating policies in chapter 5 and in the last chapter.

...and Promises

Meanwhile we want the likes of Tina. The Merage Foundation for the American Dream does its part. Each year it selects from its twenty-two partner universities outstanding, foreign-born graduating seniors to become American Dream Fellows.[16] It chooses the Fellows on the basis of their academic record, leadership, consistent ethical behavior, the clarity of their American dream, and their potential to make an important contribution to America. Fellows receive a $20,000 stipend over two years to help them pursue their dream. Consider the following idealistic students it selected in 2010:

Maria Baryakhtar, from Ukraine, Harvard University. Her dream is to obtain a graduate degree in theoretical particle physics, to conduct research, and to introduce new approaches to teaching K-12 science and math.

Kreshnik Begolli, from Kosovo, University of California, Los Angeles. His dream is to improve education in the integration of theoretical and applied research through social and cognitive science._

Abimbola Dairo, from Nigeria, Stanford University. Her dream is to expand her UCAN! Program, which targets low-income high school students who are unprepared for the college admissions process.

Ina Jani, from Albania, Northwestern University. Her dream is to obtain a graduate degree in public health and join Doctors Without Borders to serve as an ambassador for America.

Swetha Kambhampati, from India, MIT. She dreams to become a physician in academic medicine and implement sustainable medical technologies that address global health challenges._

Lindel Krige, from South Africa, University of Georgia. Her dream is to be a physician conducting clinical research while providing low-cost health care to those in need.

Cristian Martinez, from Mexico, University of California, Irvine. Her dream is to obtain a PhD in public affairs and become the assistant secretary of state for the Bureau of Western Hemisphere Affairs._

Vivekananda Nemana, from India, New York University. His dream aims to become a journalist concentrating on economic issues affecting low-income areas.

Ana Gabriela Robleto, from Nicaragua, University of Miami. Her dream is to become a physician and improve the health conditions of people in the Americas.

Maria Shpolberg, from Ukraine, Princeton University. Her dream consists of becoming a history professor, author, and leading educator focusing on the connections between twentieth century European cultural and political history._

Ye Tao, from China, Harvard University. He dreams to train as a physician scientist and serve as a public health researcher and advocate.

Yi Wei, from China, Harvard University. Her dream is to obtain a degree in planning and public policy and work to solve complex urban problems.

Shades of Tina, Jian Liu, and Lisceth Cruz. Do we want more of them? This particular group wishes to strengthen our education, nurture our inventiveness and innovation capabilities, connect us to the world beyond our borders, and commit to the value of our institutions, as it expresses its faith in the American dream. What can we do to make them permanent residents, immigrants, and citizens?

We don't want immigrants?

4

Nurturing Innovation, Inventiveness, and Creativity

～

*Closed societies have not progressed because they fence themselves off
from innovation in all respects. Let immigrants come.*

—THIERRY, IMMIGRANT FROM FRANCE

～

We regard innovation and inventiveness principally in terms of their economic, technological, and scientific consequences, but they also act as barometers of our intellectual and spiritual vitality. Both increasingly depend on education.

A powerful yen to invent has animated America's progress to world preeminence. It has spanned centuries, from Franklin, to Morse, to Edison, to the Internet, the GPS, and a myriad of current electronic devices. An equally strong disposition to innovate has converted inventions to practical uses, such present ones as search engines and social media.

In early 2009, a study by the Information Technology and Innovation Foundation, a think tank promoting innovation policies, places the United States fortieth in the world in terms of its inventive and innovative capabilities.[1] By the foundation's criteria, a mass of European countries, as well as the usual suspects—Singapore, China, and India—far outpace the United States. Another influential think tank, the Marion Ewing Kauffman Foundation, also worries about our competitive potential in today's global economy. It too focuses on innovation and entrepreneurship.

On closer consideration, the foundations don't record an actual reduction in our ability to invent and to innovate. Instead they castigate our policies that impede much stronger and faster progress. Both foundations observe how other countries, in competition with ours, sponsor much more effective policies to spur research, development, and entrepreneurship founded on innovation.

To reverse the perceived decline in the United States, both foundations advocate new policies that would open us to high-skill immigration. Implicitly these recommendations focus on who now invents and innovates in America.

Inventiveness

In tune with the views of these foundations, critics who claim that we no longer invent as before cite the increasing numbers of inventions originating in other countries. In the consequent reduction of the American *proportion* of world inventions, they see a decline in our inventiveness. But that others do well does not mean that we do badly. In 1977 the United States Patent

Office awarded seventy-seven thousand patents. In 2011 it awarded two hundred and nine thousand patents, an increase of 170 percent in somewhat over three decades. *Significantly, however, foreign-born working in this country received 24 percent of these recent patents.*

Inventiveness resides in our national genes. Since colonial days Americans have continued to invent, from the transcendent to the trivial—from the transistor to the paper clip. The nature of inventiveness has evolved over time. While Franklin, Morse, or Edison exemplified Yankee ingenuity and had no scientific training per se, today strong scientific and mathematical preparation unavoidably undergirds all research.

This evolution began in the nineteenth century during the rivalry of two of our greatest inventors, native-born Thomas Edison and immigrant Nikola Tesla. Both produced profoundly durable and consequential inventions. Edison based his inventions on infinite trial and error. Tesla, who had been academically trained in Europe, followed systematic experimentation and arrived at his discoveries methodically.

Upon Edison's death, the *New York Times* quoted Tesla about Edison: "His method was inefficient in the extreme, for an immense ground had to be covered to get anything at all unless blind chance intervened and, at first, I was almost a sorry witness of his doings, knowing that just a little theory and calculation would have saved him 90 percent of the labor. But he had a veritable contempt for book learning and mathematical knowledge, trusting himself entirely to his inventor's instinct and practical American sense." Sadly, late in life practical Edison remarked that, in retrospect, his biggest mistake was to have never respected theory-steeped Tesla or his work.

Tesla's age has arrived. We now depend heavily on highly educated talent from abroad. Our universities don't graduate nearly enough individuals with a scientific training to meet the demands of a modern economy. This educational insufficiency limits our pool of potential inventors. Hence immigrants and other foreign-born researchers increasingly fill the gaps. They contribute in complete disproportion to their numbers.

Professor Wadhwa and colleagues at Duke University estimated that foreign nationals residing in the United States appeared as inventors or co-inventors in 25.6 percent of international patent applications in 2006. This count does not include immigrants who became US citizens before filing a patent application.[2] For technological patents, immigrants file at double the rate of native-born.[3]

The inventiveness of foreign-born residents working in the United States benefits especially the research at some of our largest corporations and of our government. During the first decade of the twenty-first century, such foreign nationals contributed to more than half of the international patents filed by some large, multinational companies, including Qualcomm (72 percent), Merck & Co. (65 percent), General Electric (64 percent), Siemens (63 percent), and Cisco (60 percent). They have also contributed 41 percent of international patents in government-sponsored research.

Hence, our inventiveness depends heavily on immigration. But other countries have greatly increased their investment in research and development, and prospective educated immigrants now increasingly stay at home or migrate to venues other than the United States. Yet we can still attract. Foreign-born inventors among us cite a welcoming and culturally favorable climate that encourages their high performance in the United States:

In the US, I made several inventions in speech recognition and the man-machine interface. They are probably due to an immigrant arriving with a fresh vision and energy, which contrasts with too much baggage that many native-born carry. Because of that, they are less likely to be motivated to look for new ways. Had I immigrated to the United Kingdom or Canada, which I had considered, my inventions would probably not have occurred.

     —*James, scientist and researcher with an American PhD in electrical engineering; immigrated from Jamaica at age twenty-six, now a citizen*

America provides a freedom to do and an environment that stimulates fresh thinking. In turn, an immigrant brings a force of energy and an openness to venture something new. He finds that gradual immersion in America causes him also to question things as they are. Here I felt the freedom to pursue ideas that I originally had in Sweden but knew that I could never put into practice there. People for whom I worked in the United States encouraged me and facilitated the pursuit of my ideas. It worked and I created some novel procedures in cardiac medicine, specifically hemodynamicand metabolic assessments in radiocardiograms.

—*Lennart, MD, came from Sweden in his early twenties to do a medical residency at an American university; now a citizen*

But inventiveness alone, unless translated into innovation, remains socially and economically sterile.

Innovation

Unlike invention, which depends on methodical analysis and experimentation, innovation springs from an ability to imagine and envision change. *Invention* produces discrete and specific processes, products, machines, instruments, hardware, or software. *Innovation* conceptualizes existing inventions in novel, sometimes alternative, often unprecedented modes. It moves the economy and alters the culture (for instance, currently and radically through search engines or social media). Specific inventions often spur innovative thinking.

The late Steve Jobs personified the innovator's talent in the highest degree. He brought to the world the Mac computer, the iPhone, the iPad, and a multitude of other innovations. He invented nothing, but he saw the possibilities in existing inventions and imagined what others couldn't. He was, incidentally, but probably inconsequentially, the out-of-wedlock son of a Syrian immigrant. The fact that he grew up American certainly mattered more.

We worry about innovation, too, especially compared with China. But is our ability to innovate in decline? In 2009 *Newsweek* ran an article entitled "The Decline of American Innovation." Despite its alarming title, it actually reported about how Americans worry *about our potential decline*, not about documented decline. The article indicated that 61 percent of Americans thought that the 2009 recession diminished our ability to innovate. It reported a survey in which only 41 percent of Americans believed that the United States stayed ahead of China in innovation; that only 55 percent believed the same relative to India; and that only 32 percent thought that we stayed ahead of Japan.

But *Newsweek* also interviewed people in China. When asked if the United States is staying ahead of China on innovation, 81 percent of Chinese considered America to be ahead (though only 41 percent of Americans thought so); and 87 percent Chinese considered America to be ahead of India (versus 55 percent of Americans). The Chinese probably notice that the world massively uses recent American innovations such as the iPad, Facebook, Kindle, or photovoltaics, to name a mere few.

So should we rest and not worry about our ability to innovate? Thoughtful observers think that we need to worry. They cite various causes, from inadequate science and mathematics training in our schools, to the disappearance of creative learning opportunities for the young, to industry's short-term thinking that harms long-term innovation development. Journalist and author Fareed Zakaria, an immigrant himself, says,

> We have hoped it would all work out, and for a while it did. The seed capital from past decades was strong enough to carry us for decades. *We got talent from abroad to mask the erosion at home* [my italics]. We used financial engineering to substitute for the real thing. We borrowed to the hilt and sold each other our homes in an ascending spiral that made us all feel rich. And we kicked all the real problems we face down the road, hoping that someone else would solve them. This too has become part of

American culture, a culture that desperately needs to change if we are to preserve American innovation and rekindle the real American dream.

If a combination of these concerns has validity, the disposition of such immigrants as James and Lennart to think afresh should influence our policies. Immigrants' outsider outlook causes them to examine skeptically practices and institutions, question attitudes, challenge assumptions, and flush out the superfluous, the dated, and the tired. Through their innovative impulses, immigrants have reinvigorated our society across the centuries and fueled its optimism. When asked whether they saw themselves as agents of change and innovation, my interviewees told me:

Immigrants are innovative, both by personal temperament and in what they do. Many of us thrive in the American environment, which fires up our latent initiative and imagination. It has encouraged me to do innovative research in electrical engineering and obtain several patents. It has also stimulated me to view UC Davis in a more ambitious regional role and initiate an Innovation Hub. This initiative aims to better connect campus research with entrepreneurs, accelerate the transfer of discoveries into commercial products, and develop the local and regional economy. This also helps the university in difficult financial times.

—*Linda Katehi, chancellor of the University of California at Davis, born in Greece, came at age twenty-two; now a citizen*

If you mean innovation with a small "i," I certainly see myself as an innovator. Because change is welcome in this society, I felt free to implement many small innovations in my work as a software engineer. Cumulatively they add up, creating synergy. I also observe Chinese colleagues who feel much freer to innovate here than in China.

—*Marek, electrical engineer, emigrated from Poland with an engineering degree in 1981; now a citizen*

I certainly saw myself as an innovator in two particular aspects of my work. One was the effect of my English schooling, in which I learned problem solving by disassembling a problem in its component steps, analyzing them, and then putting it all back together again. This has greatly sharpened my problem-solving ability. As a manager at [a leading corporation], I found that young engineers and researchers working for me brought to problem solving the one technique that they had learned in their respective graduate programs. Each was hence different. I taught them to think in alternative ways, seeking other forms of analysis for problem solving. A second innovation consisted, in the 1960s and 1970s, of hiring women, who were simply not being hired for serious technical and scientific jobs. Here, too, my English experiences influenced me. At that time in England, we hired intelligent, well-educated women for responsible jobs.

    —Edward, born in England, with an English PhD in electrical engineering; came in his late twenties under a temporary working contract for a US company; liked America, stayed, and made a career in upper management at a major US corporation; now a citizen

Immigrants are agents of innovation by their very nature and we need them for that reason. Living in America has prompted me to think thoughts and take initiatives that I couldn't have possibly envisaged in England. There I would have heard all the reasons why I shouldn't, because of insurmountable problems. Of course, certain qualities in an immigrant are desirable, such as drive and intelligence.

    —Roger, software developer and entrepreneur, born in England, came at age twenty-seven; now a citizen

Yes, certainly. When you come from another culture, you can't help but think out of the box. In India, circumstances force one to be very aware of others, who crowd you into tight communities. So communicating ideas has come naturally to me, and two aspects of innovation have, in this sense, marked my work as an architect. For one, I communicate intensely with a client to make him understand my purpose and to understand his. For another, I see my work as integrating my building into the community, rather than having it stand apart as my architectural statement. Because of that, I build from the inside out, meaning that the outer shell doesn't come first, but only as a consequence of other considerations. Yet in architecture school we are taught to make individual statements. I attribute my approach to my original culture, as I blend into America by sublimating myself to the needs of the community and the priority of communicating ideas. By this, I believe that I bring innovation in architecture.

—*Anand architect, born in India, came at age twenty-six, trained in the United States; now a citizen*

The company I founded is in itself an instance of innovation, and it has, in turn, led to other innovations. I had great mentors in this country who taught me to think outside the box and find alternative solutions. This looking for possibilities, for what can be, what cannot, seeing the glass half-full, contrasts with Latin conformism. The ambient American culture encourages innovation.

—*Miguel, engineer and entrepreneur, born in Costa Rica, with an American master's degree in electrical engineering; now a citizen*

Multiple experiences support the truth of these observations. Consider famed serial innovators and immigrants Elon Musk and Pierre Omidyar. Both of them came to the United States young and acquired excellent educations. Neither invents, but both demonstrate intrepid innovative vision as they create new industries and new markets from recent inventions. Both, too, fit squarely into the immigrant entrepreneur profile, a topic I address in the next chapter.

Elon Musk, born in South Africa, decided to move to the United States as a very young man because "it is where great things are possible." He got quickly into high gear. In 1999 he co-founded PayPal (with an immigrant from Germany), an online financial service and e-mail payment company — a new idea at the time. In 2002 he founded SpaceX to build manned space craft. In May 2012, SpaceX launched the first privately built spacecraft to dock with the International Space Station and return safely to earth. It replaces a program discontinued by NASA. Musk's other ventures include Tesla Motors, which he started in 2003 and which produces ground-breaking electric cars. In 2006 Musk also started SolarCity, a photovoltaics products and services company.

Pierre Omidyar, who was born in France of Iranian extraction, also arrived young in the United States. Another serial innovator, in 1991 he co-founded eShop, an e-commerce company. In 1995, at age twenty-eight, he launched the now-famous auction site eBay. In 2010 Omidyar started an online news service in Honolulu called Civil Beat that covers civic affairs in Hawaii.

In addition to the usual immigrant traits, immigrant innovators share two characteristics: a generally strong education and awareness that the American culture accepts the impossible, the improbable and the inconceivable as merely normal. To quote Musk, "It is where great things are possible."

My personal experience confirms it. Upon arriving in a country where everything was different and unfamiliar, I found myself frequently puzzling why something was the way it was and wouldn't it work better if changed? Often I was wrong because I didn't understand the deeper reasons, but as time went on I kept introducing, sometimes unconsciously, new approaches in my educational publishing work, new ways of thinking and doing. Though often small, such changes reflected an outsider's sober look atalternatives.

Creativity

Cultural factors bear on innovation through creativity. Research by Adam Galinsky, of Northwestern University, shows that those speaking more than one language and who have lived abroad outperform others in creativity. He found specifically that these findings apply to bilinguals and to second-generation Americans.[4]

Immigrants thus bring us creativity. They delighted us in music: Victor Herbert, Irving Berlin, Sigmund Romberg, Al Jolson, Rudolph Friml, not to mention those already famous in Europe, such as Igor Stravinsky, or Arnold Schoenberg.

Dragan, from Serbia, encompasses innovation, creativity and entrepreneurship. Of creativity he brings an unusual version. An industrial designer, he has founded a studio in Silicon Valley and has achieved significant international success in a few years. For commercial clients he designs creative, but practical items. But in his publications and in his teaching he presents us with the unimaginable in arrays of fantastic, provocative designs of otherwise mundane objects. They tickle our intellect and kindle and stretch our imagination. He reminds us that, "As the barriers between possibility and impossibility become permeable, the imagination begins to soar."

I asked Dragan how he came to our shores:

I had the American dream since watching American movies in childhood in Belgrade. Everything in them seemed larger and more open. In design school, I realized that America was way ahead of the rest of the world in design. An American designer show came to Belgrade and it overwhelmed me. I decided that America was in my future. In my mid-twenties I started an advertising agency in Belgrade with partners. We did well, but all along I was thinking America. I put together a book of my designs and kept sending it to American design firms. None ever

answered until, finally, the one I had most interest in did. I received a
working visa, cut my roots, lifted anchor and came to the US.

Once here, how did it go?

At first, the cultural shock was almost unbearable, but my wife, who
is also a designer, and I persevered. After adapting, I came to see that
America would allow me to express myself fully. The American pioneering atmosphere has stimulated me. What I most like about America is
that it is free of the burden of tradition. Here you can attempt anything
you want, because anything is possible. I never wanted to work for others
and never doubted that I could do well. This caused me to start my own
business.

We don't want immigrants?

5

Spurring the Economy

We immigrants spur America's economy in multiple ways:

- Our entrepreneurial instincts create vast numbers of small busi-
nesses and large corporations. Through both, we generate wealth,
innovation, and employment.
- We arrive young. Our youth benefits the economy, most signifi-
cantly by disproportionately contributing to the public coffer.
- The educated among us bring technical and scientific sophistication.
- We moderate inflation and mostly benefit wages of the native-born.
- Our presence expands real estate markets.
- *We work, hard!*

Working Hard

Work activates the economic engine. Immigrants share one trait: a readiness to
work intensely. In this alone they stimulate the US economy. The ethic of *hard*

work, the only kind honored in this country, comes, of course, as an immigration prerequisite. Remember Delfina. Her story epitomizes immigrant hard work— that which was performed by her, but also the ethic she instilled in her daughters. I asked immigrants' children what they learned about work from their parents:

Both my immigrant parents are very hard working and this influence has defined me also.
—*Victorio, son of Filipino immigrants, physical trainer, real estate manager*

My father imbued me with his convictions: hard work, education, and ambition for self-improvement.
—*Pablo, son of Salvadoran immigrants, lawyer*

My father arrived in this country in 1914 at age eighteen from a small town in eastern Poland, then still Russia. He came to New Jersey with essentially little education but with a strong desire to work hard. And he did. He taught me the ethic of being honorable, the values of education, of responsibility, and of hard work.
—*Myron, MD, son of Polish immigrants*

My mother's life as a struggling immigrant widow has inspired me to work hard.
—*Pete, engineer, son of an immigrant Estonian widow*

My father didn't really understand how difficult it would be in America, but he is an optimist. My parents took a big risk and knew little English. They immigrated to a small town in east Texas and had much financial difficulty. Nothing seemed to work. They eventually started a Laundromat, where they worked long hours, seven days a week. My sister and I helped.
—*Paul, MD, son of Taiwanese immigrants*

My father was not well educated but a very hard worker. He did what he had to do. I learned to be that way and have become very productive.
—*Marilyn, daughter of Maltese immigrants*

They don't need to mention that this hard work far exceeded eight hours a day or the thirty-five hours a week advocated by some. Though undoubtedly "unemployed" legal immigrants exist, in over half a century in America I have never met any. I have encountered some temporarily out of work or seeking better employment or new opportunity, but none who drew on the public coffer.

How We Immigrants Enhance the Economy

Because of our disposition for intense work and driven by the indispensable optimism that our condition requires, we immigrants enhance the whole range of the economy. By extension, we add to the well-being of individuals throughout society.

Entrepreneurship.

In 2010, 204 of the Fortune 500 companies had been founded by immigrants or children of immigrants.

Foreign-born entrepreneurs mark the American economy broadly and deeply. They innovate, as we saw in the preceding chapter. They start businesses by the hundreds of thousands. Some remain small—in my town, Nicaraguans own one barber shop, Vietnamese another, Rumanians the hardware store, and Hispanics just about every gardening service. But foreign-born have also founded or cofounded some of the major American corporations, such as Levi Strauss or Bausch and Lomb in the past; or Intel, Google, eBay, Yahoo, Hotmail, PayPal, and Sun Microsystems more recently.

Each brought fresh thinking and employment. They seize on inventions and convert them into novel enterprises. Many have launched new products and introduced unprecedented behaviors, such as "Googling."

In *Immigrant, Inc.: Why Immigrant Entrepreneurs Are Driving the New Economy*,[1] authors Richard Herman and Robert Smith examine the influence of entrepreneurial, educated immigrants on the growth of our economy. They interview great tycoons but also prominent scientific researchers who parlayed their discoveries into successful corporations or participated in propelling Silicon Valley to its prominence. Smith and Herman feature exceptional individuals who have become part of America's new economic leadership.

We need them, of course. However, the great mass of average immigrants contributes even more to the economy by their acceptance of risk and by their hard work. They also bring us entrepreneurship at a less visible level. Based on the 2000 United States Census, Smith and Herman report that immigrants owned 1,436,410 businesses, about 12 percent of all businesses in the United States (roughly the proportion of the immigrant population in the United States at that time).[1]

The Marion Ewing Kauffman Foundation reports about the economic impact of immigrant entrepreneurs. Abundant data from its *Index of Entrepreneurial Activity* show how powerfully these entrepreneurs stimulate the economy:[2]

- Immigrants far outpace native-born Americans in entrepreneurship. In 2005, 0.35 immigrants (three hundred and fifty out of one hundred thousand persons) started a business every month, compared to 0.28 native-born. Since then, the proportion of immigrant-started businesses has increased further. In 2009 the immigrant rate of entrepreneurial activity stood at 0.51 and remained substantially higher than that of the native-born, which rested at 0.30.
- One in four engineering and technology companies founded between 1995 and 2005 had an immigrant founder. Most were highly educated in science, technology, math, and engineering; 96

percent held bachelor's degrees and 75 percent master's or PhD degrees.

- Their companies employed four hundred and fifty thousand workers in 2005 and generated $52 billion in sales revenue.
- In Silicon Valley, a hotbed of innovation, immigrants founded 52 percent of high-tech start-ups between 1995 and 2005.

The above rates represent approximately eighty-five thousand immigrants creating new businesses every month. Most are modest: a bakery, a beauty salon, a restaurant. Cumulatively, however, they contributed $67 billion to the economy in 2006.[3] The new businesses, big or small, attract more investment in cities, helping the cities' overall economies growth. None of that should surprise. The American atmosphere continues to vibrate with an eager propensity for risk taking, as it always has.

I came to earn an MBA at UCLA (I already had an undergraduate degree in India). I intended to look around before deciding whether to stay. After graduating from UCLA, I worked for a time in Los Angeles and then moved to the San Francisco Bay Area. After some time, I decided to start my own company. We work for medium-sized companies helping them lower their labor costs. Many reasons motivated me to stay and eventually to become American, among them and most importantly opportunity. If you work hard, you can achieve a good standard of living. For another, equality, a feature particularly striking for someone from India. I also like the freedom to live one's life any way one wants to; and the people are nice, open, tolerant and receptive.

—*Rajiv, Indian entrepreneur, arrived at age twenty-one to study, stayed, founded an enterprise, married an American; now a citizen*

As to what motivated me to start a company, America did. I would have never thought of doing it in England. Had I mentioned it to anyone, I would have heard all the reasons I shouldn't because of insurmountable problems. And, indeed, if I had tried to start a company there, I would have met with infinite obstacles whose purpose is to keep things as they are. In America opportunity beckons, and if you take the risk, people admire you for it! So I started a successful company in Silicon Valley, in which I employed one hundred and fifty highly-paid people. My company was always profitable and never in debt. I feel that I paid America back. Generally, I hope that my work as a programmer was beneficial to the economy.

—*Roger, software developer and entrepreneur, emigrated from England at age twenty-seven*

Abbreviating from Chapter I, Ariel, the young Argentine entrepreneur, "I immigrated...with the express intention of starting a software company that would have a transformative effect...During [my] earlier stay in America, I observed much greater receptiveness to technologic transformation than in any other country; also that the United States had the most favorable climate for such ventures, especially in California. I noticed an atmosphere of natural selection, which causes the best to come here and was sure that we would find first-rate people to work with. Here I also found fantastic professional ethics. My company is international, with headquarters in California and an office in Chile. We expect to be creating jobs in America."

Belma and Zermina

Annually, the Oppenheimer Funds sponsor the National Youth Entrepreneurship Challenge. Two high school students, Bosnian immigrants Belma Velic and Zermina Ahmetovic, were runners-up in 2010. They created Beta Bytes, a computer repair service for immigrant communities.

Belma and Zermina researched their market and found that 90 percent
of Bosnian households in Hartford, Connecticut, have one or more computers, and that on average they need four significant repairs annually. The
two teenagers discuss their enterprise in sophisticated business terms: "Our
niche market consists of the Bosnian community in Hartford County, which
stands roughly at fifteen thousand residents. We target [those]...who are
not tech savvy and struggle with the language barrier. Such a stable niche
market allows for successful expansion of our business. The scalability that
we propose can be achieved through multiple methods, including expansion to Bosnian communities outside of Connecticut to other concentrated
regions...The overall Bosnian population in the United States approxi-
mates three hundred and fifty thousand residents, which can bring great
success to our business if we tap into the entire population...Many other
ethnic groups...struggle with the same cultural and language barriers. We
first plan to expand to groups originating in the Balkan region and from
there follow a strategic path to tap into other markets." That would include
Latinos, and both girls are currently learning Spanish, which will make
them trilingual.

After graduating from high school with top honors, Zermina and Belma
expected to attend the University of Connecticut. In an interview, they ar-
gued for the necessity of teaching entrepreneurship in high school. "We are
the next generation...We are the lawyers, the doctors, the teachers. We need
to realize that we have to start opening up our imaginations. So many of the
other students ask us, 'Why do you get straight A's?' We look at them and
think, 'They don't know what opportunity they have—to have a career, to
make something of themselves.'

"If you have the passion and yearning to start your own business, then neither age nor financial status should come in the way...We can tell you...that we didn't have much...Our families migrated to the United States with less than $100 in their pockets. We...were given an opportunity of a lifetime, and we were going to make the best of it. It took a lot of hard work and effort...but we only achieved that by believing in ourselves. At only seventeen years old, many were skeptical of where our idea would take us, but we ended up proving not just to those who doubted us but to ourselves as well that a successful business can be run by two teenage girls."

"Being an entrepreneur alone poses many challenges. However, being a teen entrepreneur takes the meaning of responsibility to a whole new level. Time management has to be the biggest obstacle that a teen entrepreneur has to overcome. Dealing with classes, homework, sports, extracurricular activities, and work leaves little to no leisure time for ourselves...You have to learn to prioritize...With each challenge, you are becoming stronger and paving the path to success."

"We believe that our business is not just for profit, but also for community service. We are trying to assist our fellow people, as well as others who are in the same situation, by breaking the language and cultural barrier...The need that our community has demonstrated is easily filled with our expertise and passion for computers...The people in our community are proud that our generation is stepping up and doing something of importance, something that they hope their children will some day accomplish as well. Success to us means living the life that our parents have dreamt of living and taking every opportunity that we can...to better ourselves...being the first person in your entire family to attend college, and, even greater, to receive a medical degree."[4]

Some newcomers abound in especially vigorous entrepreneurial instincts. In 2005 Indian immigrants founded more companies than the next four groups of foreign-born entrepreneurs (from the United Kingdom, China, Taiwan, and Japan) combined.[5]

This entrepreneurial sprit wafting in the American atmosphere affected even me. In my sixties, I cofounded a publishing company with a native-born professor. We published college textbooks exclusively online rather than conventionally on paper. Why did I do it? Not because of aspirations to become a captain of industry but because the exhilarating culture inspired me to explore the limits of my potential—partly prompted by a typical immigrant's temperament, partly because of the atmosphere of immigrant-built America, where attempting the seemingly inconceivable beckons.

Youth. The late economist Julian Simon said that their youth is immigrants' most important effect of on the economy.[6] We do come young. Just look at the ages at their time of arrival of all the inventors and innovators interviewed for Chapter 4, or of the above-mentioned entrepreneurs. The overwhelming majority arrived in their twenties, most between ages twenty-two and twenty-seven. One outlier arrived at age thirty-five and four as teenagers.

Youth's economic consequences reach beyond commitment to hard work and entrepreneurial and innovative energies. New immigrants cluster predominantly in the youthful labor force ages, when people contribute more to the public coffer than they draw from it. The native-born, on the other hand, concentrate proportionately more in the childhood and elderly ages, periods of economic dependence. This matters, as Social Security and Medicare spending will likely rise from the current 8.4 percent of GDP to 12.5 percent in 2030. To moderate this critical economic problem, we need constant replenishment of a young working force.

Also, largely because of their youth, new immigrants move to an uncommon degree geographically and occupationally. Their mobility increases the flexibility of the economy and relieves tight labor markets.

Employment. Immigrants create jobs through their purchasing power but also through the businesses that they start. Any new enterprise implies a new source of employment. Both the small and the giant create millions of jobs in the aggregate. As mentioned above, the Kauffman Foundation estimated that in 2005 some 7,283 companies founded by immigrants generated just under four hundred and fifty thousand jobs. The National Foundation for American Policy reports that immigrants from fourteen countries in seven states founded about twenty-five small companies between 2000 and 2008. In 2008 they employed 3,674 individuals. We saw also that Roger, the English-born entrepreneur, employed one hundred and fifty highly-paid people in his modest-size company, very representative of the mass of such businesses.

Job creation by immigrants can take unexpected forms. My native-born friend Robert has a one-man tutoring service. His clientele consists entirely of children of well-educated immigrants from China, India, Turkey, and Iran in California's Silicon Valley.

Inflation. At the most elemental level, immigrants help restrain inflation by accepting modest wages. We come with moderate expectations, grateful for the opportunity. We expect to gain our place in American society through dedicated, conscientious work. Our beginning participation in the economy at lower pay cascades through the economy, keeping the prices of the less sophisticated products and services lower. We thus benefit the less affluent.

Quite true, from personal experience. I came to the United States in 1960 with very little money and no connections or meaningful acquaintances. After a couple of odd jobs, I found a more serious position: teaching languages at a small Catholic college in Pennsylvania. The school offered me a wage that provided shelter and food but hardly much more. Native-born with American degrees and higher qualifications didn't need to teach for that kind of pay, but other immigrants did. The college had instructors in mathematics, physics, and languages, all like me happy to have a beginning job in America. After a time, as we all gained an understanding of possibilities and opportunities, we dispersed. But in the meantime, we gratefully started at the salary bottom. In this we unintentionally served students who couldn't afford expensive tuitions or gain scholarships.

In *The New Americans*, the National Research Council states, "the benefits of immigration from lower prices are spread quite uniformly across most types of domestic consumers." But it also notes, "Benefits from lower prices are higher for households with very high levels of wealth and education."[7] Reasonably affluent Americans thus also benefit from the low-skilled immigrants who fill jobs such as housekeeping, gardening, eldercare, and childcare.

Giovanni Peri, of UC Davis, notes that while services of the less skilled in the United States are less costly, that is not the case in Europe, which has restricted immigration more. There, such basic services are expensive because indigenous workers can demand more for their work. That feeds arguments for restricting immigration to the United States on the assumption that low-skilled natives would accept such jobs if paid significantly more. This, however, would have inflation consequences and would not encourage low-skilled natives to upgrade their skills and move up the employment scale. I discuss the general dubiousness of such assumptions in the section "What About the Individual" below.

Real estate. By simply settling in the United States, immigrants boost the real estate markets as they increase the pool of new renters and eventually purchase new homes. Our initial wages allow us to rent perhaps a modest apartment. As we progress, we think of a home of our own—the American dream.

Esmeralda came from Mexico with her husband and baby son. Both she and her husband had limited education. They worked (very) hard, he in construction and she cleaning homes. She dismisses the hard work as being good for you and keeping you out of trouble. Initially they lived in the garage of relatives. Then they rented. Some twenty years later, they own a home that cost $400,000.

Edna emigrated from Israel with a husband, a baby girl, and scant money. They rented a modest apartment and worked—she hard, he casually. After a few years, Edna divorced her husband, who wasn't working like an immigrant, and married another immigrant. Edna taught music, very successfully, and her second husband worked in public schools. Now they've graduated from a series of rented apartments to their own home in a very nice California town.

Immigrants also revitalize hollowed-out rust belt cities, as Somalis have done in Lewiston, Maine, and Guyanese in Schenectady. They often buy derelict houses for a pittance and invest heavily in sweat equity, restoring and repainting them. Then they start small businesses—restaurants and groceries—in the now improving downtowns.

Scientific and technical sophistication. Immigrants provide a major proportion of the scientific and engineering labor force, especially at the highest levels of education. In a global economy that increasingly demands cutting-edge technological and scientific sophistication, they supply an obvious competitive advantage to the United States in the twenty-first century. In the Kauffman report above, we see a statistic worth repeating: 96 percent of immigrant founders of high-tech companies held bachelor's degrees and 75 percent master's or PhD degrees.[8]

The National Research Council describes immigration as a powerful economic force, essential to the continued growth of the American economy. The Council estimated in 1997 that each highly skilled immigrant has, overall, a positive fiscal impact of $198,000, calculated as net present value (total contributions in taxes, minus benefits received).

I live in Silicon Valley, where meeting highly-skilled, very well-educated immigrants comes easily. Master's degrees and doctorates in the sciences and engineering abound. Importantly, but not surprisingly, many of their children follow educational paths that converge with the most modern needs of our economy. So Will, the physicist from South Africa, has an engineer son.

So does Ian, the inventor and engineer from Jamaica. Miguel, an engineer himself and entrepreneur from Costa Rica, has parented four children, three of whom are scientists or engineers. Federico, from Colombia, an engineer, has threeAmerican-born sons, all engineers.

What About the Individual?

Immigrants' presence enhances the economy as a whole, but how do individuals fare? Who benefits? In particular, do immigrants' low wages *harm any native-born*? Much emotion swirls about this latter question. Evidence points to four main conclusions:

- The first is that the presence of significant numbers of immigrant workers in a community benefits the wages of native-born workers across the board.
- The second conclusion concerns the better educated native-born— those with high school and college diplomas. For them, the foreign-born presence results in modest gains. Since they constitute some 90 percent of the US working population, immigrants benefit the wages of a majority of native-born.
- The third conclusion concerns the least educated of the native work force. They constitute some 10 percent of it and suffer modest losses.
- The fourth is that immigrant and native-born workers by and large don't compete for the same jobs. This explains the limited actual effect of immigrants on the native-born wages.

Economists Giovanni Peri of UC, Davis, and Gianmarco Ottaviano from the University of Bologna studied the effect of immigrants on individual American workers by analyzing data from the one hundred largest US cities.[9] Supporting the first conclusion, they found that over the past three decades, for each 1 percent increase in the number of foreign-born workers, American-born workers saw a 0.3 to 0.5 percent increase in real wages.

Peri says, "Our work shows that cities with more diversity—more immigrants—in the work force exhibit higher productivity for the American-born employees. Want to make more money? Move to a city teeming with immigrants." Peri and Ottaviano calculate that five cities have benefited the most in this regard: Los Angeles, San Jose, Austin, Houston, and Phoenix. All experienced enormous increases in their immigrant residents over the past thirty years. Cities with little or no growth in immigration, such as Cleveland, Buffalo, and Pittsburgh, did not benefit from this phenomenon during the same time.

Standard & Poor confirms it. In a May 2012 release it reports that credit ratings of US cities with "significant immigration" improved over the preceding decade. The tax bases of these cities grew and per-capita incomes increased. Dayton, Ohio, which actively welcomes immigrants, has benefited conspicuously.

Regarding the second conclusion, Peri and Ottaviano's research shows that natives with a high school and college degree gained the most, with an increase of 1 percent to 1.5 percent of their wages. Indeed, work that demands skill or expertise remains largely unaffected by low wages paid to immigrants. Managerial, technical, marketing, or scientific jobs lay outside the sphere of low-pay immigrants. All require ability, experience, and credentials, which immigrants with little pertinent education lack.

Nor do immigrant wages affect well-educated native-born otherwise. Foreign-born scholars increasingly concentrate in scientific, mathematical, and technologic professions. "As a consequence, they do not harm wages in law, education, and the social sciences, where most native-born Americans thrive," Peri says. Government jobs go by examination, their wages regulated by union contracts.

As to the third conclusion, Peri and Ottaviano found that native-born workers without a high school degree experienced a wage loss of 1.2 percent. David Card of UC, Berkeley, and Jorge Borjas of Harvard have also studied the consequences of low immigrant wages on earnings of the lowest paid native-born. Card finds that the effect on wages of the low-skilled native-born workers is "modest" (and agrees with Peri and Ottaviano about the effects on wages of the educated).[10] Borjas' models project a more negative effect on the wages of the least educated native-born. While they disagree in these findings, Card and Borjas agree that immigrants' low wages affect mainly two populations: native-born high school dropouts and illegal immigrants. *Thus all researchers conclude that the effect of immigrants on native-born wages depends on educational levels.*

The fourth conclusion seems surprising. When critics assert that the foreign-born reduce domestic wages, they miss the reality that immigrants, by and large, don't compete against domestic workers for the same kinds of jobs. Most immigrants have either very little or quite substantial education and skills. Most domestic workers fall somewhere in between. Peri and Ottaviano note that immigrants add a variety of new services in cities. These services *complement* existing domestic services. This limits competition and reduces downward pressure on natives' wages. Peri also sees "job displacement"—the process by which native workers move up in the employment scale as lower skilled immigrants enter the economy—as an additional factor in the lack of direct competition.[11]

My teaching experience illustrates this principle. Our college occupied an inflation-containing market niche, well below the Ivy League or other institutions that paid better salaries to more qualified faculty, native or immigrant. It catered to students of modest means, charged modest tuitions, and hired a mostly marginal labor force. Our native-born faculty had low academic qualifications, either no PhDs or still working on them. My young office mate taught American history and worked on a PhD. Neither of us had an effect on salaries of those with higher qualifications. But we kept costs low and provided an admittedly less-than-stellar higher education. The better and more ambitious of our students transcended our limitations and went on to graduate education elsewhere.

Red Herrings

They take our jobs! We hear much lamenting about the death of bipartisanship in Washington. But when it comes to inflicting harm on our national interest, bipartisanship does quite well. Thus Democratic Senator Byron Dorgan explains why he opposes allowing more *legal* immigration:

> I don't think you need a professor to understand that when you import substantial cheap labor, it displaces American workers.[12]

Former Republican Representative Tom Tancredo said,

> I'm not going to aid any more immigration into this country. I reject the idea, categorically, that there are jobs that, quote, 'No American will take.' But am I going to feel sorry if a business has to increase its wages in order for somebody in this country to make a good living? No, I don't feel sorry about that and I won't apologize for it for a moment. And there are plenty of Americans who will do those jobs.

Other senators concur: Republican Charles Grassley, Democrat Dick Durbin, and Socialist Bernie Sanders, among others, have opposed an increase in granting H-1B visas (a program that allows American companies and universities to hire highly skilled foreign scientists, engineers, and programmers). Such nativist politicians happily support the beliefs of a substantial portion of the electorate, who think that immigrants take our jobs and burden our social services.

In that spirit, Congress has mandated that the US Geological Survey can hire only American citizens. As recently as the 1970s, it could hire the best geologists from around the world.

But do they? If "they" take "our" jobs, could it be that "we" are not qualified for the jobs on offer or may not want to take them because they don't pay enough in our opinion? *The Wall Street Journal* reported in August 2010, at a time of a 9.5 percent unemployment rate, that many Americans refused jobs that seemed not very desirable to them.[13] These jobs required qualification and competence, such as blue collar mechanics. Those refusing the jobs were uniformly native-born, not immigrants.

Sentiments opposing immigration lead to stagnation over competition, to immobility over progress. They ignore the massive evidence of benefits brought to us by useful, economy-stimulating legal immigrants. Predictably, immigrants scorn such arguments as bogus. Responding to the question "As an immigrant, have you taken a native's job?" they say:

Of course, not. There are no "American jobs." There is no right to jobs. One has to earn them.

—*Miguel, Costa Rican, engineer and entrepreneur*

Nonsense. Of course I didn't. Competition improves our society and immigrants challenge and improve us.

—*Anand, Indian, architect and entrepreneur*

No, I haven't. No American would have taken my initial jobs at the wages I was paid. I am a legal resident and take pride in never having taken a dollar from the American government. Instead I have given, by paying my taxes regularly and conscientiously for twenty years. I have held a steady job with the same American boss for nineteen years and still work six days a week. Also, my son is an American Marine.

—*Joaquin, Salvadoran, gardener*

This is laughable. Competition is just stiffer now. The world of easy jobs has disappeared and we need to develop new skills to adjust.
  —*Elisa, Korean, MD*

No, certainly not. No immigrant does. There is opportunity for everyone.
  —*Peter, Estonian, engineer*

Never. I always had a good job because I believe that it is a matter of a can-do attitude. There is always work available and I always found some, never in competition with anyone else that I was aware of.
  —*Roger, English, engineer and entrepreneur*

I haven't. We all earn a job here; those who do it well, keep it.
  —*Yvonne, Vietnamese, corporate executive*

No, of course not. I was qualified for every job for which I was hired. Speaking Spanish has also helped me and so has working hard.
  —*Margarita, Mexican, nurse*

The benefit of the doubt. Silvana, Italian immigrant and a corporate executive in California, says in response to whether she had taken a native's job:

> No, I haven't. In America, if you are better, you get the job. For an immigrant it is more difficult in any case because for good jobs you need references and immigrants typically don't have them. On the other hand, you are often given the benefit of the doubt.

I agree with Silvana. I came to the United States bereft of any contacts and recommendations. For every job I was offered, I was given the benefit of the doubt. Coming from less open-minded societies, it left me constantly amazed. Doesn't the same open-minded generosity of spirit apply to native-born workers?

H-1B visas harm American workers? Those H-IB visas, opposed by the above senators, stir virulent debate. Donna Conroy, a grassroots lobbyist and executive director of BrightFutureJobs.com, details in her website how companies are dismissing US citizens from their jobs in record numbers to replace them with H-IB foreign workers. She advocates a movement to stop the legislation that allows H-IB visas.[14] The Feb. 24, 2010, *Lone Star Iconoclast* echoes Conroy:

> SANTA BARBARA, Calif.—Large corporations in the United States are laying off American workers by the thousands and replacing them with foreigners who have been assigned an H-IB nonimmigrant visa. According to authorities, these visas can usually be obtained quicker than a US green card since it is the company that must make application.

Conroy's and the *Lone Star Iconoclast*'s concerns fail to note that the H-IB controversy stems largely from our educational deficiencies. As we saw in Chapter 3, we don't graduate nearly enough students to satisfy the scientific and technical demands of a modern economy. The *San Francisco Chronicle* (Aug. 3, 2011) throws a different light on the H-IB controversy:

> Competition for cloud computing engineers, security experts, and mobile developers, as well as sales professionals in the technology industry, has gotten so fierce in the past six months that companies are going to greater lengths to woo prospective employees...For companies, this means an increase in labor costs as salaries rise and businesses try to retain workers with perks and retention bonuses.

Hard to see how H-IB visas threaten American jobs. Current policy caps at 117,000 the annual number of H-IB visas in an economy of about 6 million high-tech American jobs. Meanwhile, the National Foundation for American Policy reports that 24 of the 28 immigrant parents of 2011 Intel Science Talent Search winners started working in the United States on H-IB visas and later received an employer-sponsored green card. I have more to say in Chapter 9 about the importance of H-IB visas.

We don't want immigrants?

6

Becoming American

~

Citizens Now!

My citizen swearing-in ceremony was quite emotional. There were several hundred of us in a huge hall. I saw faces from around the world, Asians, Latin Americans, Africans, Middle Easterners and some Europeans. When we raised our hands to be sworn in, tears were running down many faces and I, too, felt deeply moved.

—ROGER, IMMIGRANT FROM ENGLAND

~

Many immigrants, though far from all, eventually make a full commitment to the rest of us by becoming citizens. A majority of new Americans probably share Roger's emotions. When I ask them what they like about America, the words *opportunity* and *freedom*, in that order, come first in most cases—words that define their American experience.

Who becomes a citizen and who doesn't? The United States Census Bureau reported in 2009 that 12.5 percent of the US population was foreign-born—some 37.5 million people. Of them, only 43 percent had become naturalized citizens by 2009, amounting to 16.8 million new Americans (an improvement since 1996, when only 37.5 percent of foreign-born were naturalized). Thus some 57 percent of current immigrants show no interest in becoming citizens.

Ethnicity matters and the desire to naturalize varies considerably by region of origin.[1] Of Europeans, 61 percent became citizens; so did 58 percent of Asians and 56 percent of Caribbean migrants. From other parts of the world, only 32 percent have done so. Mexicans, the largest foreign-born group, have very low rates of naturalization: only 22.6 percent became naturalized by that year.

So less than half of the foreign-born become full-fledged Americans. What of those who don't? The Center for Immigration Studies provides some conclusions[2]:

- Higher levels of education correspond to higher rates of naturalization. Immigrants born in India are twenty-two times more likely to be college graduates than Mexican immigrants. Indians also naturalize at much higher rates than Mexicans. But Mexicans in professional or managerial positions are almost twice as likely to naturalize than their laborer compatriots.
- Higher skill occupations correspond to higher rates of naturalization.
- Higher household income corresponds to higher rates of naturalization.
- Immigrants who speak English well are more likely to become Americans.

- Immigrants living in married couple households are more likely to become citizens.

As a gross generalization, then, the 57 percent are the less educated, especially if Mexican.

Why some become citizens. The 43 percent who become citizens may do it from idealism or from calculation; their commitment to the United States may be full-hearted or conditional. I have asked my interviewees what being American meant to them.

Becoming a citizen did affect me…it elevated my thinking about the participatory process of democracy. I do have my doubts about democracy sometimes, but it is clearly better in a lot of ways than oppression. I always vote gladly. I reference Plato in my involvement with my church parish councils and the administration of volunteer groups. Plato said, "One of the penalties for refusing to participate in politics is that you end up being governed by your inferiors." I find this profound and amusing at the same time.

—*Ghassan, immigrant from Syria, father of two American-born, college-educated daughters*

We decided to integrate right away and now, when we go to Poland, we are strangers there to a degree. Living here has made us Americans in more than formal citizenship. We made a conscious effort to assimilate, learn the language, and become responsible parts of society. We consider being American a privilege and an obligation. Because of that we also consider it our duty to vote.

—*Anna and Marek Sikorski, immigrants from Poland, parents of a son and a daughter born in America, both college-educated*

I became a citizen for all the reasons I like America: that anybody can become anything, so different from Europe; that people welcome you very quickly; that they are open and they engage. At some point I decided that there is no way I would go back to France. I vote because there are so many countries where you can't.

    —*Thierry, immigrant from France, parent of two American-born children*

I took to America like duck to water, liked its culture and found myself easily absorbed into the New York melting pot. I became a citizen as soon as I legally could because I felt that the United States was now my home. I vote because I want to participate. The feeling of inclusion that voting gives me is important.

    —*Tim, immigrant from England, with two American-born children*

I am an active, engaged citizen. Ten to fifteen years ago I hesitated about that, but not anymore. I vote because it allows me to participate and because I feel that my vote counts.

    —*Ahmed, Pakistani immigrant, parent of American-born, college-educated son and daughter*

I came to the United States in 1964 to study accounting. Here I met my future, American wife; we have two children. As I became a legal resident, I began to understand how American life enriched me. I valued freedom of speech, which does not exist in Iran. Mostly, I valued the freedom of choice. I also observed how Americans always come up with solutions. For instance, in the early 1980s, when things looked so bad, Americans pitched in and turned the country around. I realized that I wanted to participate, to vote and affect my new society. This led me to become a citizen. Looking back, I have not the least regret about having immigrated. Can't think of anything about America I don't like.

    —*Rick, Iranian immigrant*

None mentions two magic immigrant words: *dream* and *determination*. Soraya, another Iranian immigrant, personifies both.

Soraya

I came to America as a teenager and alone. While an adolescent in Iran, I dreamed of life in America. I saw it as the land of opportunity, where I would have freedom of choice and could make my own decisions. When I graduated from secondary school in Tehran in 1986, Iran was at war with Iraq and there was no freedom or good prospects. I decided that it was time to act on my dream, and I made my way to Turkey, which had an American embassy (as there wasn't one in Iran). Getting an American visa became relatively easy: I am a female, hence presumably more trustworthy; had top grades in my secondary school; my uncle, an earlier immigrant living in California, provided an affidavit for me; and I had received an admission acceptance from a college in California.

So I arrived in California in 1987, knowing the little English I had learned in school. Bewildered by the extraordinary differences with my home country, after a few months I moved to Minnesota to be closer to the family of another immigrant uncle, who was a successful businessman in Minneapolis. I registered as an undergraduate at the University of Minnesota. To support myself, I tutored in mathematics and chemistry. After graduating, I entered the School of Pharmacy, where I obtained a doctorate degree in due time. While a student, I met my husband, himself an immigrant from Turkey, where he was a physician. He came to the University of Minnesota to obtain a PhD that would allow him to do research in his field.

I see myself as an average immigrant and I did what immigrants do. I studied and worked very hard in my initial years and ever since. It wasn't always easy, but I am not a quitter and I persisted till I reached all my academic goals.

I say to immigrants who may be inclined to drop out: 'Don't give up.' After our graduations in Minnesota, my husband and I decided to move to California because it offered good opportunities, for him to practice and teach, for me to work professionally. In California we still worked and studied just as hard, since both of us had to take the California Boards. Because of the need to establish ourselves, we waited ten years before having children. I worked as a pharmacist, and when I became pregnant I quit and am now a fulltime mother of two sons, ten and six years old.

Life in America hasn't disappointed my dream. I am a citizen now because I consider the United States my country. Most of all I appreciate democracy, freedom, and opportunity, and I vote because it counts. I volunteer in the community by, for instance, collecting food for the poor. It makes me happy to volunteer. Living in America has caused my thinking to evolve in ways I don't always appreciate. I have changed religions, which would have never happened in Iran.

Soraya and all these other well-educated new citizens state full commitment to our civic life. Through their multiple influences and by how they bring up their children, they bear disproportionately upon our future.

Assimilation and integration. These positive voices notwithstanding, 57 percent of newcomers exhibit a tepid commitment to learning English, to adopting our customs, and to eventually becoming citizens. Nor did my less-educated immigrant interviewees articulate strong citizenship impulses. Each individual decision differs, however, from every other.

I have been an American resident for forty years but have not become a citizen yet. Initially my avoiding citizenship reflected political circumstances in my homeland. By now, however, it is just negligence on my part. I intend to become a citizen.

—*Ilona, highly educated immigrant from Hungary, mother of an American-born son*

In the current resistance to further immigration, assimilation and integration play a major role. Sofia, granddaughter of Greek immigrants and a dedicated high school teacher, thinks that we should control further immigration until we have assimilated those migrants already in the country. Several immigrants and offspring of immigrants I interviewed agree with her. As we saw in Chapter I, many native-born opposed to further immigration share her views as well. Assimilation and integration have become a political issue and will influence any immigration policy we shall evolve.

How they vote. Not all new citizens feel the same degree of engagement as those positive voices above. Their voting behaviors illustrate different levels of commitment to our civic life.

By voting, we express participation in our society and in our political system. How the new Americans vote takes particular meaning in light of so many natives who regularly do not (some 40 to 50 percent don't vote, though they did better in 2008). The California Voter Foundation provides results of a statewide survey on the attitudes of infrequent voters and of citizens eligible to vote but not registered.[3] These predominantly native-born claim that they are too busy, that special interests control our politics, that candidates don't really speak to them.

But even when they vote, some don't do it meaningfully. My friend Robert tells me that in 2008 he voted for himself because he found no candidate compelling enough to deserve his vote. He felt a citizen's duty to vote, if only symbolically. Overall, such natives hold a sour view of America.

Because of their often intense feelings about having become Americans, one would expect naturalized citizens to vote for all the reasons expressed by my interviewees. Not all do. The Sikorskis feel it their duty to vote. Others vote for reasons that amount to a collective endorsement of our political system and of our culture.

Elisa came from Korea at age fourteen. The daughter of a Korean MD mother, she is an MD herself, married to an American MD and mother of two American-born daughters. She told me:

I vote because it counts, in contrast to what happens in Korea. In fact, I press my husband to do it also. Though he is the grandson of immigrants, he seems to disdain this fundamental civic duty.

Bertha, a twenty-year-old student at the University of California and immigrant from Liberia, votes as well, because:

I enjoy the American system and all that's positive about America. I am a citizen now and I vote because this is my home and I believe in America.

Pascual, a young Dominican immigrant and computer programmer, has equally strong reasons to vote:

I am a citizen now and I vote, partly because I believe in the ideals upon which this country was founded, that all men are equal and have the same rights.

Other new citizens shirk this civic duty. The November 2008 election illustrates degrees of engagement:

- The United States Census Bureau reports that 71.8 percent of *native citizens* of all races registered and that 64.4 percent voted.
- Of *naturalized citizens*, only 60.5 percent registered and only 54.0 percent actually voted that year.

• Some ethnic groups of *naturalized citizens* show a stronger predisposition to vote. Thus 59.4 percent of blacks among them voted; 55.6 percent of whites did, as did 54.2 of Hispanics, but only 49.1 percent of Asians voted.[4]

Naturalized citizens leave something to be desired. They registered at a lower rate than the native-born and also voted significantly less. The Census Bureau rates *all* voters, native or naturalized, in terms of their schooling. Those with less than a ninth grade schooling education voted at a 23.1 percent rate; those with progressively greater education voted at increasingly higher rates. Thus, 72.4 of college degree holders voted, as did 77.3 percent of those with an advanced degree. My educated interviewees certainly support this finding. They make better citizens.

Whether well-educated or not, naturalized citizens and their children—the second generation—make a profound difference in our civic engagement. Though only 16.8 percent of US citizens, these two generations provided 54 percent of new voting registrations between the 2004 and the 2008 elections. They also supplied 44 percent of the increase in voters. Such degree of civic engagement by these new citizens and their children should matter to us greatly—especially when considering that only a third of American adults can name all three branches of government and a third can't name any![5]

How They Mark America

Becoming a citizen carries immediate civic consequences and generates long-term, far-reaching effects.

In the short run, having found their bearings, the new Americans begin to blend into our culture and institutions. As they harvest the fruits of their labors, assimilate, and acculturate, they inject renewed vitality into our society. They participate in their communities and they vote. Some stand out by their influence across all domains of our national life: famed educators, innovators, scientists and inventors, politicians, artists, and entrepreneurs. The work of myriad anonymous, ordinary new citizens, though less visible, marks our lives even more. Cumulatively, they break down tired and dated structures and flush out timeworn, pessimistic, sometimes negative attitudes.

Many Americans worry that immigrants destabilize our culture. Data disprove it. Consider alcohol abuse or drug use. Conclusions from the 1999–2001 National Survey on Drug Use and Health suggest that immigrants are much less likely than natives to indulge in substance abuse. Data for alcohol show use by 72 percent of natives versus 53 percent of immigrants. For tobacco the respective statistics are 32 percent and 22 percent. For marijuana they are 5 percent and 2 percent, and for drugs, 6.6 percent and 3.2 percent.[6]

Over the longer run, the new Americans modify our society across generations. Most raise their children as Americans, but Americans with an enriched and enriching cultural twist. Often these children become at least as well or better educated than their parents. (Also see below, "Consider Culture in Its Broadest Sense," and the next chapter.)

In 2011 the nation's leading public university, the University of California, Berkeley, enrolled 5,253 incoming freshmen. Of them, 70 percent had at least one parent born abroad. We can expect these students to rise in society. Over time, the descendants of immigrants in the second, third, and fourth generations move into positions of leadership, joining and gradually altering our elites.

Turning Over the Elites

The few, the "elites," lead all societies. Only in America the few keep changing. In a characteristic, almost exclusively American social condition, immigrants, or mostly their immediate descendants, constantly renew our elites.

In 1971 I moved to Boston from then dynamic, venturesome California. I thought of Boston as the home of the Yankee founding fathers and early

American civic leaders. But that year I found no Yankees in Boston politics—no Cabots, Everetts, or Lodges, not in Boston or anywhere else in Massachusetts. Instead, in 1971, Boston's mayor was an Irish-American, as had been his predecessors for a number of years. Moreover, the Boston City Council consisted of thirteen Irish-Americans and one Italian-American. I wondered what happened to the Yankees.

Over time I understood that I witnessed in Boston an essential aspect of America's historical course: the movement into positions of leadership by descendants of immigrants. The traditional New England establishment, perhaps tired, certainly outnumbered, had retreated, replaced by the more ambitious. (As of this writing, incidentally, Thomas Menino, an Italian-American, has been Boston's mayor since 1993.)

In the United States in general, our initial elites consisted entirely of Anglo-Saxon, mostly English settlers. Our emerging elites come from around the globe. See the Irish, German, Italian, Russian, Jewish, Chinese, Indian, and Hispanic names among the leaders in all domains of our society. They inherited the energy and attitudes of their immigrant parents and grandparents.

Classless America. In societies divided by classes, the rich and the powerful inherit privileges and entrenched positions *impermeable to outsiders*. In some countries, one could not imagine moving upward into wealth and power. Even in democratic Western Europe, traditional outsiders, domestic or immigrant, find it difficult if not impossible to break into the established power structures.

By contrast look how America allows easy succession and constant renewal of the casts in its political, economic, and cultural elites. It's because we have no classes. We have instead transitory economic *strata*, the members of which fail to reach the category of a permanent establishment. America's classlessness constitutes a principal attraction for us immigrants. Here the rich, the not so rich, and the poor churn up or down the socio-economic ladder in constant turnover. The very rich have children who drop out of their "class." True, some often parasitic people remain in the wealth stratum for an extra generation or two, but the essentials of our culture demand effort and renewal—the bane of classes.

Consider politics. The United States Senate looms as the quintessential bastion of elitism. But in America elitism fluidly finds new channels. In 2010 30 percent of senators, most of them quite wealthy, descended from non-WASP, often very modest immigrants: thirteen Jewish; three Irish; two each Japanese, Italians, French, and Poles; one each black, Croatian, Serb, Slovene, Cuban, and Greek. That year 40 percent of the representatives in the House also descended from non-Anglo-Saxon immigrants. Also in 2010 nineteen governors out of fifty were not WASPs: one East Indian, three Italians, four Irish, two Poles, three Germans, one half-Mexican, one Jewish, two blacks, one Scandinavian, and two more were immigrants themselves, a Canadian and an Austrian. Of course, Presidents Kennedy and Reagan stemmed from those formerly undesirable Irish. In recent decades, we find no descendants of the Founding Fathers, or of any US presidents—no Roosevelts, no Adamses.

Consider economic power. Twenty-four DuPont heirs appeared on the 1982 *Forbes* list of the four hundred richest people. By 1999 no DuPonts made the cut, but a third of those listed were either immigrants themselves or descendants of recent immigrants. Members of the *Forbes* list change from year to year. Some drop out, others rise. Elites measured by wealth turn over mercilessly here. No Vanderbilts or Fisks make the list anymore; instead you see tycoons descended from recent immigrants, like Michael Bloomberg or Larry Ellison. Of course, *Forbes* now lists outright immigrants Pierre Omidyar and Elon Musk, serial entrepreneurs and innovators (whom I discussed in Chapter 4). In fact, ninety-seven outright immigrants have appeared among the four hundred richest people over the past twenty-five years.

Consider modern, scientific, analytical knowledge. Harvard political scientist Robert Putnam wrote in 1977, "If the dominant figures of the past hundred years have been the entrepreneur, the businessman, and the industrial executive, the 'new men' are the scientists, the mathematicians, the econo-mists, and the engineers of the new intellectual technology."

Immigrants do their part. Since 1901 one-quarter of all American Nobel Prize winners—eighty of them—were immigrants. This number does not include children and grandchildren of immigrants, which added an even larger number of American Nobel Prize winners. Others, not Nobel winners, matter as much or more—for instance, Jonas Salk, grandson of immigrants, developer of the polio vaccine.

Consider culture in its broadest sense. Intellectually influential journal-ists Thomas Friedman, David Brooks, and William Kristol descend from Jews, which were reviled a century ago by nativists because of fears that they would subvert our culture. Scholars descended from Italians, Russians, Greeks, Japanese, and infinite other nations staff our universities by the many thousands.

Composers Leonard Bernstein, George Gershwin, and Aaron Copland have defined our national musical idiom. Very shortly after landing in the United States, I heard the urgent rhythms and the vast, sweeping melodies of George Gershwin's "Concerto in F." I thought, "Oh! America! Yes!" I toiled at the time as a longshoreman in the port of New York.

New men and now women, mostly second and third generation Americans, often well-educated and cosmopolitan, continue to infiltrate bul-warks of the established. Why does it matter? In thriving societies, elites con-sist, at all levels, of the capable, the energetic, and the dynamic. The United States has remained a classless, meritocratic, and mobile society because of the constant replacement of its elites. By contrast, in devitalized societies elites tend to entrench themselves into a class system, impervious to constant renewal.

Holland teaches an object lesson. It had one extraordinary century, es-sentially most of the seventeenth. That era produced an incomparable ava-lanche of talent, inventions, and innovations. Amsterdam gave birth to modern capitalism (first stock exchange, first multinational corporation: the Dutch East India Corporation). In science and in technology, the Netherlands marked important advances. Leeuwenhoek, tradesman and scientist, invented the modern microscope and laid the foundations of microbiology. The great mathematician and physicist Christiaan Huygens invented the pendulum clock. Another inventor perfected the powered sawmill. This allowed the Dutch the massive construction of the world's best ships and the most powerful navy of the day. In turn, this led small Holland to its great maritime empire. The resulting Dutch Golden Age wealth sponsored a veritable explosion in the arts (Rembrandt and manifold other great painters). Intellectually Holland also left a mark. Hugo Grotius essentially founded international law; great, internationally influential publishing houses arose; foreign philosophers found welcome in Holland.

It all started with immigrants. At the beginning of its age of preponderance, especially after 1585, Holland benefited from a large wave of immigrating talent. Merchants and artists came from what is now Belgium to escape religious persecution; for the same reason, so did French Huguenots, German Protestants, and, a little earlier, Sephardic Jews from Portugal and Spain. They found a liberal society and blended in with the open-minded natives to create a new country, receptive to all, with no hereditary social classes. But after one hundred years, the Dutch genius ran out of steam. No more outsiders brought new energies and ideas. Not then, not since. In recent decades the Netherlands have admitted some refugees on humanitarian grounds, but no great talents like those in the sixteenth century have knocked at Holland's door. Dutch society, prosperous and pleased with itself, became increasingly rigid, solidifying into social classes. Over the subsequent three centuries, it settled into a genteel and sophisticated well-being, its great creative energies exhausted, with a few occasional exceptions. John Adams, though he meant it admiringly, said that we had much to learn from Holland. Indeed.

Individuals can attain power or influence through inheritance or through ability. Societies in which leaders prevail predominantly or exclusively through inheritance tend toward stagnation, followed by decline. Holland rose through ability, but after a century, its elites lapsed into inherited privileges. Decline never occurred thanks to Dutch ethics, but neither has growth taken place. Talents still knock on America's door. Let's heed the Dutch lesson.

Where leaders attain power and influence through ability, societies generally experience more felicitous destinies. Leaders may, of course, possess ability, but not morality. Such societies can become tyrannies. In countries where the law rules and where leaders are allowed to emerge through hard work and talent as in America, meritocracy becomes the norm.

Nurturing the rise of leaders through merit rates as an obvious national priority. But turnover in positions of leadership becomes increasingly difficult in a rapidly maturing United States, as layer upon layer of the privileged continue to reach for power through their wealth. More often than is good for us, they do it through connections and inheritance rather than through intrinsic merit and energetic performance. Holland discontinued immigration once it became prodigiously successful. Shall we also?

We don't want immigrants?

7

The Second Generation

Their American-born children—the second generation—are immigrants' most valuable bequest. As these children grow into fully developed, modern Americans, most enrich our national life out of all proportion to their numbers.

- The second generation often excels in education.
- Commonly it inherits and practices an ethic of hard work and self-reliance.
- Often bi- or trilingual, it brings a cosmopolitan perspective and creative talents.
- With few exceptions, it views America as promise, not as disappointment.
- The immigrants' descendants transform America's elites.

Most of the second generation learn the positives of our culture from their parents: work, law, community, and self-improvement. Often worldly, they expand our reach, transcend our mental and geographical borders, and spread our influence across the broader world. The second generation also contains a small but harmful minority of noncontributing and even bad citizens. How their foreign-born parents bring them up determines much of their eventual place in American society.

Forming the Second Generation's Character

In our exceedingly affluent society, many American parents struggle with the need to develop a strong character in their children. In an extensive article in the *New York Times Magazine* ("What If the Secret to Success Is Failure?" Sept. 14, 2011), Paul Tough examines the importance of teaching character. Tough features two high school principals: Dominic Randolph of Riverdale Country School and David Levin of KIPP Charter School, both in New York. Private Riverdale Country School caters to a prosperous class of educated parents. KIPP educates the very poor and the educationally disadvantaged.

Both schools excel in educational standards and performance. Just about all their graduates go on to college, but both principals have concluded that their otherwise excellent respective academic programs don't always lead to eventual student success. Both principals have become convinced that character building needs to complement educational excellence. They have created programs that divide character education into two categories: programs that develop "moral character," which embodies ethical values like fairness, generosity, and integrity; and those that address "performance character," which includes values like effort, diligence, and perseverance.

Much more often than not and by the very nature of the immigrant experience, immigrant parents bring up the second generation in both aspects of character building: moral and performance. I asked some second geners (a new term) how their foreign-born parents had raised them and what effect that had on them as adult Americans:

Myron, physician, son of a modest Polish immigrant:

"My father was the greatest influence on my life. He came to this country at age eighteen from a small town in eastern Poland with essentially little education but with a strong desire to work hard. He taught me the ethic of being honorable, the values of education, responsibility, and hard work. When he immigrated, his goal was not to become rich, just to live a life of sufficiency, and in this he succeeded. From him I also inherited my priorities, among which becoming rich was not important. I expect nothing that I haven't earned or not achieved on my own. I also believe that I must return to society what it gave me: the opportunity to achieve. I am happy to report that I have been successful in transmitting some or much of that to my son, the 'third generation.' By the fourth generation it's all lost. They begin to expect and to demand."

Olga, medical student, daughter of educated Russian immigrants:

"My parents were privileged in the Soviet Union but had to scrape a living here. They taught me how to treat others, how to be sensitive to them, taking interest in them and in their life stories. I also learned Russian warmth and sincerity. I learned languages but also cultural differences and peoples' emotions. Watching my mother make steely, necessary decisions under very difficult circumstances has affected me. Mother baby-sat initially, my father tried to teach tennis. Their struggle to become successful developed in me a sense of purpose, ambition, and a feeling of being driven."

Michelle, graphic designer, daughter of educated Italian immigrants:

"My parents' initial struggles taught me and my siblings the importance of strength of character. We also received a thorough exposure to Italian culture. Our parents taught us to appreciate the arts, to be practical, to appreciate the family, to want to be educated. Their influence has descended to my children, who are bilingual (as my husband and I are) and whom we take periodically to Italy to give them exposure not only to that culture but also to a broader understanding of the world."

Edwin, graduate student at the University of California, Berkeley; son of a Haitian mother, a teacher, and a Jamaican father, an engineer:

"There was a constant emphasis on education. It was understood that my parents expected my brother and me to excel educationally, though they didn't micromanage us in this regard. It was expected that I would go to college. Additionally, my mother taught me that my objective should be to help people."

Pablo, lawyer, son of educated Salvadoran immigrants:

"My father imbued me with his convictions: hard work, education, and ambition for self-improvement. He aimed to make me acutely aware that I am American and to ask myself, 'Am I a good American?' My mother, I realize now, has provided me with moral foundations to make me honorable. I think that my parents achieved their combined goals in bringing up my siblings and me."

Amelia, high-level administrator in the University of California system, daughter of modestly educated Mexican immigrants:

"My parents brought an immigrant perspective. Seeing how hard they worked for us, their children, sometimes two shifts in a day, created in me a very strong desire to succeed. I myself went to work at age sixteen and a half and also worked through college. I have succeeded in America thanks to my excellent parents, who taught me the values of family, religion, morality, and respect for education. They succeeded in giving all their children a good education; we all went to college. I went to Stanford. My brother excelled in mathematics, became an engineer, and went through ROTC. We experienced some discrimination, but we are all citizens and my parents are very patriotic Americans. I see myself now as an architect of change. In my work I aim to change my mostly second-generation students' lives based on my own experiences."

Consider *Nnamdi Asomugha*. He was born in New Orleans, the son of Nigerian immigrants, his father a petroleum engineer and his mother a pharmacist. He is also one of the very best cornerbacks in the National Football League—so good that opposing quarterbacks have learned not to throw the ball to receivers he covers. For his valuable services he receives very high wages. Unlike so many of his colleagues, he sets an example of laudable activities off the football field through extensive involvement in philanthropy—not only through donations of money but also by personal engagement.

His parents brought up Nnamdi strictly in Los Angeles (not an easy place to be strict). They made him and his siblings read instead of watch TV. His three siblings have earned graduate degrees. *Time* reports (Oct. 3, 2011) that "the Asomughas would regularly visit homeless shelters and lead food drives…Today Nnamdi chairs two philanthropic programs. One supports vocational-skills training, business loans, and health care for orphans and widows in Nigeria. The other takes a select group of inner-city students on spring tours of colleges like Harvard, Howard, Georgetown, and NYU."

Nnamdi's upbringing doesn't seem unusual. I asked immigrant parents how they brought up their American-born children.

Miguel, engineer and entrepreneur, immigrant from Costa Rica, describes his adult children as bicultural, optimistic Americans with a cosmopolitan outlook. His wife and he taught their three boys and one girl that they are not entitled to anything but need to earn it. They have endeavored to expose their children to the outside world as early as possible through travel and the study of other cultures. Their children are well-educated and love music, but Miguel still tries to stress the importance of being contributing citizens by voting. He taught them also that if you are not failing, you are not trying hard enough. "We have aimed to make them creative and innovative entrepreneurs, though one became a college professor."

Ahmed, engineer, immigrant from Pakistan, is married to an educated immigrant from Mexico. They have raised their now adult son and daughter in the values on which they themselves had been brought up. Ahmed specifies hard work and responsibility but also respect—for their religion (both children are Muslim) and for elders. He considers his children completely American and hopes that their upbringing will make them good Americans and not compromise on their principles.

Mercedes, a Mexican migrant with little education but with strong convictions and moral clarity, hopes that her children will be examples of good values. She spent much time in conversation with them and has taught them the importance of education, respect, and discipline; that nothing is given and that you have to earn it; and the importance of the family. She says that her children are "now all right," but that she had to combat adverse elements of the American environment: too many choices and the temptation to shirk responsibilities. "I am trying to counteract these influences by explaining the difference between limited choices in Mexico and life in the United States."

Once more, *Delfina* (from Chapter 2), thinks that her daughters have been greatly influenced by the difficult immigrant lives of their parents. They raised them as Americans, but Delfina thinks that they are different Americans. She brought them up strictly and taught them her values of morality and compassion: that you don't deserve anything, that you work hard, and that you must earn everything. Delfina thinks that they practice these lessons, are responsible and hard working, and don't assume that they are entitled to anything.

Farzaneh, Iranian immigrant, a small business owner, has two daughters, both college graduates. One works in high technology, the other owns a dance studio. Farzaneh and her husband taught them that they are not entitled to anything, that everything must be earned, and that they should work hard. Her daughters speak hardly any Farsi, and Farzaneh considers them completely American.

Esmeralda and her husband are Mexican immigrants with little education. Esmeralda reports that in raising their three sons she aimed to instill responsibility. She fought the influences of the American environment, which causes adolescents to have damaging expectations and demands. She allowed no TV and no computer games until the boys had completed their homework and no dating until they graduated from high school. She also never stopped talking to them about what matters in life. Two have graduated from college and the third is still in high school. She reports proudly that the two older sons, now married, have thanked her for the upbringing she gave them.

Whether Nigerian or Pakistani, Mexican or Costa Rican, Iranian or Nicaraguan, Russian or Italian, well-educated or not, immigrant parents concur in what they teach: an ethic of hard work, the value of education, the morality of being entitled to nothing except what we earn. Such upbringing produces results across the entire spectrum of American life.

Some immigrant progenitors reach across more than one generation. I asked three third-generation Americans about contacts with their immigrant grandparents.

Sofia, the granddaughter of Greek immigrants, teaches high school. So do her two daughters, the fourth generation. Uncommonly, all three teach the most at-risk teenagers—high school dropouts to be rescued or adolescents with mental, social, familial, and psychological problems.

> *You and both your daughters teach the most difficult of high school students. How much of this rare dedication can you attribute to the influence of your grandparents?*

A great deal, in fact. They formed my mother's and my worldview and character through their powerful moral and spiritual personalities. They caused us to respect the importance of work and that you have to earn what you have. They received no help from anyone and made it on their own, even though they arrived poor and with little formal education. We observed their life struggles and strength of conviction and I think that there is a direct thread, descending from them, which runs now into a fourth generation. They taught us to be kind and to help others, to have compassion. I think that we grew up with a sense of mission, which I was able to transmit to my daughters, who continue to practice the traditions and values of their great-grandparents.

Bill, retired business executive and grandson of Polish immigrants:

> I was fortunate to have known well all four of my Polish immigrant grandparents. They were amazing persons. They formed my behavior as a person and as a citizen. I learned lifelong lessons from them: responsibility, how to treat others, respect for the elderly, and the centrality of the family. Every other Sunday the entire family would gather for dinner, an important memory of my childhood. Both my grandfathers had skills, one mechanical, the other agricultural. They never ceased teaching me those skills. They were factory workers and took pride in the work they did.

My grandparents developed my sense of citizenship. They were dignified people who would never accept charity and who expected to make it on their own. They valued greatly being American citizens and considered voting a must because there was no voting in Poland. They were highly law abiding because they came from a land where the law wasn't observed. Under their influence I have become a patriotic, voting American, proud at the same time of my Polish heritage.

Jerome, university professor, grandson of Eastern European immigrants:

I think that my father inherited from his immigrant parents a fantastic work ethic and a desire to succeed. He attended Cooper Union at night for seven years to earn a degree in chemical engineering. These characteristics in turn passed on to me and to my brother. Both of us have done quite well.

Education

More often than not, children of immigrants excel educationally. Some 28 percent of Americans hold a bachelor's degree, but of the second geners I interviewed, 100 percent do. All my interviewees, educated or not, with children still in elementary or secondary schools told me that they intend to have their offspring go on to college. All the middle-aged immigrants with only a grade school education themselves report that their children had graduated from college and that several had obtained postgraduate degrees.

Spectacular results confirm such anecdotal impressions. The Cato Institute reported in 1995 that first and second generation immigrant children did unusually well in school. They won an astonishingly high proportion of scholastic prizes. In 1989 they were valedictorians in thirteen of seventeen Boston public high schools. That year 55 percent of Westinghouse Science Talent Search finalists were first- and second-geners.[1]

By 2011 this trend had accelerated. In that year's Intel Science Talent Search (successor to the Westinghouse) *more than 70 percent* of the finalists were children of immigrants. The Intel Search also reveals that in 2004, 60 percent of the top science students in the United States and 65 percent of the top math students were born to immigrant families. The *San Jose Mercury News*, (Jan. 26, 2012) reports that 2012 Intel Science finalist Jin Pan, age seventeen, son of Chinese immigrants, has written "a computer program to identify how quickly a protein chain is created and identified where the formation of proteins pauses. That discovery could improve the yield in biotechnology research and help improve computer simulations of protein formation. Pan's research could someday contribute to more effective vaccines."

Most of these high performers probably had educated parents. But many children growing up under dire conditions, of uneducated parents and frequently of single mothers, succeed against the odds because America also redeems. In *Exceptional Outcomes* (see also Chapter 3), the editors Fernandez-Kelly and Portes describe striking instances of educational success under very adverse conditions—Horatio Alger stories of children of the uneducated and of an often dubious legal status. Some *Exceptional Outcomes*[2]:

> Miguel Morales, son of poor Mexicans, has earned a BS in physics with honors at the University of California, San Diego. He followed that with an MSc in physics at San Diego State and is now working on a PhD in computer science.

> Raquel Torres, daughter of equally poor Mexicans, has earned a BA at the University of California, San Diego, with a 3.0 GPA. She went on to obtain a master's in education at San Diego State. She now teaches.

Ovidio Cardenas, son of uneducated Cubans, has obtained a PhD in molecular and cellular biology at John Hopkins University.

Alberto, another son of little educated Mexicans, came to the United States at age twelve. He has earned undergraduate and graduate degrees in engineering and added an MBA, all in the California State University system.

G. Cristina Mora, daughter of poor Mexicans, earned a PhD at Princeton University and now teaches at the University of California, Berkeley.

Parental education, culture, and ethnicity. *Exceptional Outcomes* lists dozens more such successes of offspring of struggling newcomers. It recognizes them as exceptions and concludes that most children of uneducated immigrants fail to achieve a college education. Among the parents interviewed in *Exceptional Outcomes*, expectations of college graduation ran very high in all instances, especially among Filipinos and Vietnamese. But success eludes many, and parents' education and culture seem to matter especially.

Both factors have deep consequences. *Exceptional Outcomes* reports that on high school math scores Taiwanese, Chinese, Japanese, Vietnamese, Filipinos, Argentines, and Chileans achieve the highest results, whereas Mexicans, Laotians, Cambodians, Haitians, and Dominicans achieve the lowest. The spread in reading scores narrows but remains consistent. Taiwanese score highest (716), while Cambodians lowest (530). The overwhelming majority of the low-performing ethnicities also descend from parents with low education.[3]

The above math and reading scores correlate well with second geners' college graduation rates. Among Chinese, 42 percent graduate from college; 45 percent of Filipinos do; but Nicaraguans graduate at a 32 percent rate; Cubans and West Indians at 20 percent; Haitians at 9 percent;

Vietnamese at 7 percent; Mexicans (despite all those listed above!), Laotians, and Cambodians score lowest at 2 percent.[4]

All these results largely correspond with the level of the parents' education. The General Social Survey, which tracks data since 1972, confirms that only 45 percent of children with parents who have less than a high school education go on to college (not necessarily graduating). Of children with parents with more than a high school education, 67 percent go on to college.[5]

Throughout, *Exceptional Outcomes* points to the sway of the immigrants' native culture on their American-born offspring. A moving story, "Here's Your Diploma, Mom!" relates the efforts of Stephanie, born to an uneducated Haitian single mother. To honor her mother's tremendous exertions for survival, Stephanie worked her way through high school with a grade point average of 4.25 (on a 4.0 scale yet!). Upon graduation, she enlisted in the Army. She is now a college student.[6]

I read this and think of her mother and of the culture she instilled, perhaps unconsciously, in her daughter. Indeed, the Children of Immigrants Longitudinal Study reports that 85 percent of Haitian children in south Florida had graduated from high school in 1995–1996. An extraordinary accomplishment in the face of handicaps their parents confronted: 35.5 percent without high school education themselves, an average family income of $16,394, non-English-speaking, prejudice against blacks. Modest Haitian migrants, sturdy Haitian culture. Did we know? (But note above, when it comes to college it doesn't carry over, as only 9 percent of the Haitians' second generation graduate from college.)

Ethic

Though probably not believed by current opponents of immigration, newcomers commonly arrive with a desire to work hard and, through self-reliance, earn their place in society. Their American-born children inherit these beliefs. In interviews with immigrants about what they teach their children, the importance of education regularly appears but surprisingly religion practically never. Instead, morality and responsibility recur, as does the obligation to work and to earn, rather than an expectation to receive.

> My father was not well-educated but a very hard worker. Would do what had to be done. I learned to be that way and have become very productive. I also learned not to be frivolous, not to feel entitled to anything, to have moderate expectations, and that I must earn everything I got. I think that morality was central to my upbringing. I have transmitted these values to my three children. They are now grown and have children of their own, but I am proud to say that none of them are in debt because I taught them how to be responsible—it came down from my father.
>
> —Marilyn, *daughter of modest Maltese immigrants*

Meiying, an educated Chinese immigrant, speaks about how she instills ethics in her two American-born children:

> I aim to develop certain essential qualities in them, with particular stress on responsibility. The surrounding culture operates against responsibility, as exemplified by TV and video games. They set children against their parents. I teach discipline, respect for elders, compassion, kindness, giving, listening; also ethics, which ultimately has a spiritual component. I also develop their work ethic. Even though they are only fourteen and twelve, they have been working for the past year and half for a Mexican farmer, handling his stall at the farmer's market. They have complete responsibility for the selling and for the management of the money. The farmer leaves them alone to handle the stall. Among other advantages, this exposes them to the working class and to interacting with the public, as well as being ethical in money management.

I also teach them not to be competitive against others but to have high expectations of themselves, to reach their full potential, to be humble and to observe, to know when to lead and when to follow.

Cosmopolitan Temper

The globe has flattened and the United States continues to play the preeminent role in it. Increasingly we need to interact knowledgeably with rising and declining countries and understand all the quickly changing opportunities, risks, and demands they represent. Yet most native-born show no interest in other countries, let alone in world affairs; they have never traveled abroad and speak only one language.

In 2006, during America's wars in Afghanistan and Iraq, *National Geographic* revealed that only 14 percent of young adult Americans could find Iraq or Iran on a world map, only 58 percent were aware of Afghanistan, and only 17 percent could find it on the map. During political debates in the fall of 2011, a leading presidential candidate appeared never to have heard of Uzbekistan and demonstrated confusion about Libya. None of that seemed to dent his support among portions of the electorate. According to surveys, only 18 percent of Americans, most of them concentrated on the two coasts, own a passport. Presumably a majority of naturalized citizens own one (I certainly do), which diminishes further the portion owned by native-born, especially in the heartland.

All this appalls and dismays us, the new Americans. When I asked otherwise mostly enthusiastic new citizens what they didn't like about America, many deplored indifference to the outside world, as in this sample:

Look at the TV programs people watch. They are just not interested in anything. We are also not coming to terms with our evolving identity. Who are we and what is our place in the world after the collapse of communism?

—Polish immigrant

I was shocked at how ignorant Americans are. No knowledge of geography or of other cultures. I had expected sophisticated people in a country as advanced.

    —Iranian immigrant

Americans are very provincial and don't care about the rest of the world.

    —another Iranian immigrant

...mostly appalling ignorance, generally, and of the world especially.

    —Mexican immigrant

...uninformed about the outside world and no interest in correcting that.

    —Jamaican immigrant

...ignorance of history and of the world.

    —Vietnamese immigrant

...ignorance of and lack of interest in the rest of the world. That ignorance is a subset of a general national arrogance vis-à-vis the world. This results in foreign policy disappointments, such as the war in Iraq, or dealings with Iran.

    —Indian immigrant

...most Americans don't appreciate their country. I would require that all eighteen-year-olds work for two years in a foreign country, then return and find out how they feel about America.

    —English immigrant

We can no longer afford such provincial attitudes in a rapidly integrating, interdependent world. As an antidote, many immigrants, certainly the educated, bring up their children with a cosmopolitan outlook and expose them to personal experiences of foreign countries.

Anand, the American-educated Indian architect, says that he and his Indian wife have taught their American son honesty, hard work, and the value of education, on the whole values both Indian and American. Anand observes that though their son leans towards friendships with Indians, he has turned out to be a cosmopolitan American. He is self-reliant and self-sufficient, and an individualist rather than thinking of family first, as an Indian would.

Zoia, an educated Russian immigrant, has two American-born offspring, he a lawyer/judge, she an artist. Both evolved naturally into becoming Americans, but also, Zoia thinks, different in that they have absorbed their parents' outlook. Neither is materialistic. Both put others first and are hard working, well-educated, and very cosmopolitan. Zoia and her husband exposed them to languages: Russian as children and then to French and German, respectively, when both their children did postgraduate work in Europe.

Meiying, the Chinese immigrant, sees herself as cosmopolitan rather than as Chinese or American. Her mother brought her up that way. Because of that she raises her children with a cosmopolitan outlook. She expects that this will make them worldly, influential Americans, comfortable in other cultures across the world. In that spirit, she teaches them critical judgment—for instance, to be skeptical of solely what American media tell them. Some second geners join the Foreign Service as a consequence of their worldly upbringing. Pablo, a lawyer, son of educated Salvadorans, of course bilingual, works for USAID in Nicaragua.

Civic Engagement

The second generation varies in degrees of civic engagement, in many instances as the by-product of their cosmopolitan inclinations. Their attitudes can range from a strong faith in American institutions to a rejection of the United States. Ultimately, their often emotional decisions, influenced by their parents' native cultures, reflect very personal views, tinged, in many instances, with a degree of ambivalence.

Earlier second generations committed more fully. Their parents arrived often uneducated, impoverished, and rejecting their native countries. Their children, in turn, seeing first-hand how much their parents' destinies had improved in America, generally felt a ready and full commitment to the land of their birth. Now geopolitical circumstances have changed. Most legal immigrants arrive much better educated. They feel less inclined to disown their original cultures, and they bring up their American-born children with greater positive awareness of those cultures. Often these parents are "inter-migrants," prone at some point to return to their native land or to retire there. Hence they may be less motivated to breed the intense American patriotism in their children that earlier immigrants did.

Pablo, the lawyer who works for USAID, exemplifies the highly committed and cognizant: "I grew up in Chicago, but in both worlds—United States and El Salvador. As a result, I think I am more aware of being American and what that means (I identify with El Salvador only mildly). Because I was exposed to two cultures I think that I am different from natives of a more conventional background. This is a big advantage. It makes me understand what it takes to be an American. As a result I am more consciously patriotic in examining my country and in assessing its faults and merits. My father escaped El Salvador's dictatorship and corruption. When I see elements of either in America I am particularly sensitive to them. It makes me able to question whether America lives up to the promise of its ideals. I am more wary of bad government and a better patriot for questioning authority."

Guido, an equally well-educated son of well-educated Italian immigrants, offers a more modulated view: "I see myself as an American only somewhat different from most descendants of rooted natives. My upbringing gave me a more cosmopolitan outlook, both internationally and domestically. I am perhaps less jingoistic about America, more aware of other societies, and because of that more analytical of our own. This is important in a mature country that has become resistant to change. It needs exposure to other ways, which opens minds."

Other second geners range on a spectrum. Their immigrant parents sense it.

Ahmed, a Pakistani immigrant, has two adult, well-traveled, and trilingual children. Though they are half Pakistani/half Mexican, he finds the cultural and civic decisions thoroughly American.

Iranian immigrants *Muhammad and his wife* say that their two adult Muslim children are like any other Americans, though perhaps more analytical than those of native parents. Their daughter is very logical, very bright, but critical of America. Their son is not different from other Americans, but he opposes what he perceives as anti-Muslim policies and attitudes.

Linda, a Greek immigrant, doesn't perceive her two adult sons as particularly American, more bi-cultural and cosmopolitan, equally comfortable in America and in Greece and in that sense modern. They understand how soft power in the modern world operates, and she sees them as ambassadors for both countries.

Esmeralda, the Mexican immigrant with limited education, reports that she and her husband taught their three sons to ignore their ethnicity. Nevertheless, all three are bilingual and both American and Mexican. Esmeralda expects them to become responsible Americans, bent on improving themselves.

Miguel, the Costa Rican entrepreneur, says, "We brought up our now adult children as bi-cultural Americans. We gave them as much exposure to the outside world as possible through early and frequent travel. I see them as optimistic Americans with a cosmopolitan perspective. They are well-educated and love music, but I am still trying to stress the importance of being contributing citizens by voting."

But *James,* immigrant from Jamaica, has a son and a daughter born in this country. His son, an engineer, does not identify himself as American, holds a Jamaican passport, and has recently migrated to Europe. His daughter remains excited about life and opportunities in the United States.

What these ambivalences mean to us. James' son renounces his American identity, while others express degrees of criticism and ambivalence. Does that harm us? I doubt it. These young adults will in time mature. As they do, they may evolve in their self-perceptions. When James's son begins to internalize his life among Europeans, he may discover that they perceive him as more American than Jamaican. Regardless of hesitations about their Americanness, such second geners still bring cosmopolitan perspectives to us and export to the world the soft power of our attitudes. Give them time!

Creative Drive

Second geners witness their parents, to whom everything often seems possible, and this rubs off, sometimes unintentionally, sometimes deliberately.

Certainly, Miguel, the Costa Rican Silicon Valley entrepreneur, feels that he has successfully inculcated entrepreneurial drive in three of his adult children.

Salman Khan fits the pattern. He synthesizes the best of the second generation's mark on America: commitment to education, initiative, and the ability to envision and enact change.

Salman was born to a Muslim family in New Orleans, his father from Bangladesh, his mother from India. Salman became valedictorian of his high school class and holds three degrees from MIT: a BS in mathematics and a BS and an MS in electrical engineering and computer science. To that, he has added an MBA from the Harvard Business School.

In late 2004 he began tutoring his cousin, Nadia, in mathematics over the Internet using Yahoo!'s Doodle notepad. When other relatives and friends sought his tutoring, he decided to distribute his tutorials on YouTube, where he created an account in November 2006. His tutorials' popularity on the videosharing website and the testimonials of appreciative students prompted Salman to quit his job as a hedge fund analyst in late 2009 in order to focus on developing his "Khan Academy" full-time.

Each of his videos attracts on average more than twenty thousand hits. Students from around the world have flocked to his concise, practical, and relaxed teaching method. This method also enhances classroom instruction. Secondary schools in California's Silicon Valley increasingly adopt the Khan method for their math classes. There, his videos allow each student to study at his or her individual pace and the teacher to act comfortably as a personal tutor for each student's separate learning needs.[7]

In Chapter 4, I speak about innovation arising from imagination and vision, about how a given invention can become a transformative innovation. Salman Khan personifies these qualities. He describes his purpose as

"...to accelerate learning for students of all ages. With this in mind, we want to share our content with whoever may find it useful. With so little effort on my own part, I can empower an unlimited amount of people for all time. I can't imagine a better use of my time." His videos now reach isolated areas of Africa and Asia. He also plans to extend his "free school" to cover topics such as English and history: an instance of second gener creativity.

Salman Khan's creative talents fit a broad pattern among second geners. It appears that multilingualism, which most often accompanies a cosmopolitan outlook, carries an interesting companion: creativity. As mentioned in Chapter 4, the research by Adam Galinsky, of Northwestern University, indicates that speaking more than one language and having lived abroad raises one's creativity. He found these conclusions specifically applicable to bilingual second geners.[8] Multilingual myself, I consider this unsurprising. Every language develops the words it needs to reflect the particular angle of its worldview. When confronted with the unfamiliar, our arsenal of words expressing the same from different viewpoints and varying angles allows us to envision alternative perspectives and perhaps creative solutions.

Not All Is Light

The United States Census Bureau calculates that thirty million second-generation Americans were born since 1950. Not all of them exhibit the positive characteristics described so far. Small minorities have remained ignorant, become criminals, or rejected our society in drastic ways. We need to examine them to understand a negative side effect of immigration.

The salient fact: alienated and noncontributing second geners overwhelmingly, but not exclusively, descend from uneducated, poorly acculturated, and often illegal migrants.

They fail in education. We see above that some groups of second geners don't perform as well in their education as others. Such deficiencies concentrate among children of uneducated parents and in certain ethnicities.

Exceptionally elevated high school dropout rates mark such students (particularly "Hispanics," with 17.6 percent, versus a national overall rate of 8.1 percent).[9] Social consequences follow: these eventual citizens don't contribute much to the economy and remain mired in its lower reaches. The younger males, as they seek to escape their socio-economic condition, may join gangs or engage in crime: such are sadly second gener Mexican gangs in San Jose, Salvadoran Maras in Los Angeles, or Somalis in Lewiston, Maine.

They contribute to crime—or not. Many Americans mistakenly attribute high criminality to immigrants. Facts contradict such impressions. The overall US incarceration rate stands at 3.51 percent. *No immigrant group reaches that mark* but their children often do, as Table 8.1 indicates.[10]

Table 8.1: Incarceration rates

Ethnicity	Percent incarcerated, males ages 18-39			
	Nativity		High school graduation	
	Foreign born %	US born %	No %	Yes %
Indian	0.11	0.99	1.20	0.14
Chinese, Taiwanese	0.18	0.65	1.35	0.14
Korean	0.26	0.93	0.93	0.34
Filipino	0.38	1.22	2.71	0.41
Vietnamese	0.46	5.60	1.88	0.55
Salvadoran, Guatemalan	0.52	3.01	0.71	0.62
Mexican	0.70	5.90	2.84	2.55
Colombian, Ecuadorian, Peruvian	0.80	2.37	2.12	0.74
Laotian, Cambodian	0.92	7.26	2.80	1.04
Cuban	2.22	4.20	5.22	2.29
Dominican	2.51	3.71	4.62	1.39

Let's observe Table 8.1. Even the worst immigrants fall well below the overall US incarceration rate of 3.51 percent. In fact, the average incarceration rate of all immigrants is 0.68 percent. The most numerous group, the much criticized, often illegal Mexicans, turn out to have rather low criminality (0.70 percent). *By the second, US-born generation, however, criminality rises spectacularly, especially among high school dropouts.* Does that mean that immigrant parents fail to bring up their children responsibly? Even the worst second gener criminality rate (Cuban dropouts, at 5.22 percent) doesn't make that case. It suggests that 94.78 percent of Cuban parents meet their basic social obligations.

Education also matters in another sense: the five least incarcerated migrant ethnicities come from Asia. Note the influence of high school graduation, e.g. among Indians, Chinese, and Taiwanese (0.14 percent). Asians happen to contain the largest percentages of educated newcomers. The highest rates of incarceration occur among migrant groups with the least education. Cubans form a special case. The first wave came around 1960, mostly well-educated and predominantly from the middle class. Subsequent waves arrived from other layers of Cuban society (e.g. Marielitos).

Filipinos show a fairly high ratio of high school dropouts, but of all immigrant groups, their children also feature the highest percentage of college completion (45.5 percent, versus the overall US population's 28 percent). Filipino parents also have the highest educational ambitions for their children: 92.2 percent expect them to go on to graduate schools. Table 8.1 shows categories of concern, but its generalities cannot condemn entire ethnicities. Every Mexican woman with low education I interviewed had made sure that her children graduated from college (for instance, Esmeralda, above).

Some feel alienated. Table 8.1 does not address a distinct antisocial phenomenon: the harsh alienation from the United States among certain second geners. Regularly in recent years, the media report potential terrorist plots by native-born. The suspected perpetrators are overwhelmingly young Muslims. Though their numbers are minuscule—no more than a few dozen individuals—their suspected actions carry a strong emotional impact on public opinion following 9/11.

This phenomenon, stoked by US government actions that affect Muslim sentiment here and abroad, may fade over time. The practical, if not the emotional, consequences of this alienation may be negligible. The current number of Muslim immigrants in the United States cannot be assessed objectively, but a variety of sources estimate it at about a million. They originate in South and Southeast Asia and in Arab countries. Those who intend to express themselves violently constitute probably no more than 0.01 percent of Muslim second geners and practically none among the newcomers. These numbers suggest that the great majority of Muslim immigrant parents act responsibly.

A milder form of second geners' alienation takes the form of political non-engagement. Of those born *before* 1980, 31 percent have not bothered to register to vote as of 2008. Of those born *after* 1980, however, only 18 percent have not registered. This causes optimism. Latinos represent by far the largest portion of the nonregistered second geners (24 percent).[11]

On balance, the second generation's positives far outweigh the negatives.

We don't want immigrants?

8

Balancing Our Population Growth

Too Many of Us or Not Enough?

As we grope toward a new immigration policy, we need to take the measure of our demographics. There are now three hundred and ten million of us. That seems like too many, not only because multitudes stress all our resources, clog freeways, and cause many other adversities, but for a more important reason. As we multiply, each of us loses a measure of individuality. We become more anonymous; our neighborhoods and our communities lose a personal feeling. The antisocial dissolve more easily into invisibility. Government grows because ever larger numbers of us require more services, more identifying, more control, more laws. We become ciphers, known by the nine digits of our Social Security numbers.

Some favor further population growth on the theory that it will stimulate economic growth. Is the putative economic gain worth the loss of our individual voices in politics? The House chamber of Congress still has four hundred and fifty-three seats. Each House member now presumably speaks for six hundred and eighty-four thousand constituents. Can he or she hear you or me? When I immigrated in 1960, the US population stood at one hundred and seventy million, and each member represented three hundred and seventy-five thousand voters—already too many. A California senator must now listen to thirty-eight million voters. When I settled in California in 1961, there were already nineteen million.

None of that promotes a healthy civil society or democracy, and NumbersUSA, an anti-immigrants lobby, agrees:

> The 1990s saw the biggest population boom in United States history. This is truly astounding news coming three decades after widespread agreement among Americans that the country was mature and probably already overpopulated. No wonder Americans became increasingly alarmed at their deteriorating quality of life due to sprawl, congestion, overcrowded schools, lost open spaces, and increasing restrictions on their individual liberty caused by the new population explosion!

Incidentally, for this state of affairs NumbersUSA blames government policies that favor legal immigration.

Yet I advocate more immigrants. How can I justify that? The unbalanced nature of our population growth presents us with a dilemma. Our present *native-born birth rate* is low. Our *native-born fertility rate*, predictor of our future, falls slightly below the population replacement rate. We teeter on the brink of demographic decline. This would seem good (down from three hundred and ten million), but it isn't. A society that declines demographically has too many aged and too few working-age young to pay for the retirement and health care needs of retirees. Societies in demographic decline also lose optimism, drive, and civic commitment.

To retain a youthful, dynamic, optimistic society, we need to fine-tune our population balance through carefully calibrated immigration. Immigrants, educated or not, share one characteristic: their youth and, hence, fertility.

The Appendix below provides demographic data and explanations. They lead to some broad conclusions. One, that generally immigrants are more fertile than the natives. Another, that the less educated the newcomers, the more fertile. Immigrants can rebalance our population mix and raise its fertility to a replacement rate. But that requires some tradeoffs—therein the dilemma.

Our Options

To stabilize our population at a replacement level, which do we want: the uneducated but fertile or the educated but procreating below the replacement level (Table 2 below)? We need both: the educated for their powerful effect on our education (Chapter 3) and on our economy (Chapter 5); and the less educated because their fertility raises our overall fertility to the desirable replacement level (Table 3 below). As a countervailing factor, the second generation's fertility rates decrease sharply, correlating with improved education and income.[1] This finding seems to apply equally to progeny of the well-educated as to that of the less so.

Of the sixty-six married immigrants I interviewed, 62 percent have two children, 15 percent have three children, and another 15 percent have one child; one person has four, another seven, and another none. This group yielded a ratio of 2.1 children per couple. Overwhelmingly, these immigrants are educated, hence their fertility rate registers at just the replacement rate—not that one can draw conclusions from so small and informal a sample.

While increase in education tends to deflate fertility, the inherent optimism of American society has the opposite effect. We see it in Table 3 in the total fertility rate of sending countries. At home, it averages 2.32; in America it rises to 2.86. We see it in Table 1 in our overall fertility rate of

2.06, contrasting with much lower rates in European countries, where gloom over their future prevails. These statistics result from cultural optimism, an immigrant import since our very beginnings. Optimism remains anchored in our culture, fed regularly by hope-bearing newcomers. Pessimists don't emigrate.

> Immigrants bring energy and optimism—the cultural identity of Americans.
> —*Linda, immigrant from Greece*

Their youth also benefits us demographically. Young women arrive in their most fertile years and behave mostly in accordance with the findings of Table 3. Albert Saiz, of the University of Pennsylvania, estimates that if we sustain our current immigration rates, by 2050 immigrants could provide two-thirds of the population growth in the United States.

Immigration has other demographic effects. It has made up for population losses in some parts of the country. In New England and the Mid-Atlantic, the labor force would have declined from 1990 to 2000 without immigration.[2] As we add immigrants, we need to keep a careful demographic eye on the different aspects of their impact. So much to weigh when deciding on a finely tuned immigration policy that serves the national interest.

Appendix - The Demographic Data

The Centers for Disease Control (CDC) reported in 2003 that in a continuing twelve-year decline, the US birth rate had dropped to its lowest recorded level, including a new record low for teenage births.[3] Our birth rate fell to 13.9 per 1,000 persons in 2002, from 14.1 per 1,000 in 2001, and from a peak of 16.7 per 1,000 in 1990. By 2009 that birth rate had fallen further to 13.8 per 1,000 persons. CDC analysts attribute these declines to the increasing life span of Americans, which results in a smaller proportion of women of childbearing age.

A *birth rate* represents numbers of births in a given period, such as a year. A persistently declining birth rate suggests that we may not reproduce fast enough to maintain a stable population level. The *fertility rate* estimates the expected number of children born to a woman over her child-bearing years. It assesses demographic prospects over a span of years and predicts our future. When fertility stays at around 2.1 children per woman, it has reached a *replacement rate*, which allows a population to remain stable. Anything lower than 2.1 fails to replace the existing population. Anything higher projects a population growth in excess of mere replacement.

Consequences. Falling birth and fertility rates lead to damaging social consequences. The Population Reference Bureau explains what happens to countries whose population falls below the replacement rate.[4] In Italy, the working-age population will shrink by 20 percent between 2005 and 2035 and a further 15 percent by 2050. In Japan, the twentysomethings work-force, its best educated ever, will dwindle by a fifth in the decade ending in 2020. Much of the Northern Hemisphere, including most of Europe, Russia, China, and South Korea, faces these conditions.

The shrinking pool of their working-age populations has become a drastic problem for these countries. In addition to losses of skills and knowledge, the most harmful effects descend on those older than sixty-five. Low birth and fertility rates jeopardize pension guarantees and long-term health care programs for retirees. State pensions systems face difficulties now, when in some countries four people of working age remain to support each retired person. By 2030, Japan and Italy will have only two per retiree; by 2050, the ratio will be three to two. Worldwide in 1950, twelve persons of working age labored for every person over sixty-five. By 2010, that number had shrunk to nine. By 2050, it is projected to drop to four.[5]

Aggravating these trends, medical breakthroughs continue to raise life expectancy in all industrialized countries. The European Commission estimates that demographic changes may push up public spending by between 5 and 8 percent of gross domestic product by 2040. Taxpayers will resist footing that bill. An ageing, shrinking population poses problems in other, surprising ways. The Russian army has had to tighten up conscription because of a shortage of young men.

Our Prospects

All this can happen to us. But though our birth rate trends lower, our fertility rate encourages. Table I shows how we compare with our economic peers and rivals.[4]

Table I
Birth and fertility rates in industrialized nations

Country	Birth rate 2009 (CIA)	Fertility rate 2010 (CIA)
United States	1.38	2.06
France	1.25	1.97
China	1.40	1.54
Russia	1.11	1.54
Canada	1.02	1.58
Spain	0.97	1.47
Germany	0.81	1.42
Italy	0.81	1.32
Japan	0.78	1.39

The American fertility rate, which at 2.06 almost reaches the 2.10 replacement level, largely offsets concerns about our low birth rate. Because of that, we stand in a relatively better demographic position than just about any industrialized nation. By contrast, all other countries in Table I not only suffer from low birth rates but also from discouraging fertility rates, particularly Spain, Germany, Italy, and Japan.

Still, the United States falls short of the desirable 2.10 level. Nor is it assured to remain at even its present level. The Center for Immigration Studies (CIS) reports that the current US *native-born* fertilty rate approaches 2.0 children per mother.[5] As our core population ages and lives longer, this insufficient fertility rate, if not invigorated, will likely decline. Given this already fraught fertility rate of native-born mothers, what explains the 2.06 rate in Table I? *Immigrant women do.* They supply the .06 difference between the native born 2.0 and the 2.06 in Table I.

In fact, the *characteristics of our immigrants* explain the fertility difference between the United States and the other countries in Table I. Our newcomers are not only significantly more numerous but also much more varied by ethnicity, culture, and, increasingly, by level of education, in which they far surpass the average immigrant to those other countries.

Fertility: Native and Immigrant

Without the addition of immigrants, the US fertility rates would not reach the 2.06 rate in Table I or the desirable replacement rate of 2.10. The CIS supplies the data for Table 2, which shows how the fertility rate of immigrants exceeds that of US native-born, in some respects considerably.

Table 2
Fertility rates of US native-born and of immigrants[6]

	Fertility rate
U.S. high school drop outs	2.3 children
U.S. college graduates	1.8 children
Immigrants lacking a high school degree	3.3 children
Immigrant college graduates	1.9 children

Table 2 highlights the direct relationship between education and fertility. Both native-born and immigrant high school dropouts have higher fertilities than their college-educated counterparts. As a nation, we aim to reduce the numbers of high school dropouts and increase those of college graduates. Hence, the longer trends in the fertility rate of native-born should decline from their current 2.0 rate in any case. Can immigrants continue to push our fertility rate up to the desirable 2.10 replacement level? That appears to depend on education. If we favor less educated immigrants, this should help keep our demographic trends in balance.

How does newcomers' fertility evolve once they settle in America? We can glean some answers from the data in Table 3, which consists overwhelmingly of non-European countries. They are our future population, as they already are California's.

Table 3
Immigrant fertility rates in US[7]

Country	Fertility Rate in home country	Fertility Rate in US
Mexico	2.40	3.51
Philippines	3.22	2.30
China	1.70	2.28
India	3.07	2.23
Vietnam	2.32	1.70
Korea	1.23	1.57
Cuba	1.61	1.79
El Salvador	2.80	2.97
Canada	1.51	1.86
United Kingdom	1.86	2.84
Total fertility rate of sending countries	**2.32**	**2.86**

After settling in the United States, the total fertility rate of sending countries stands at 2.86. Very encouraging when compared with the current 2.0 rate of the native-born. Though most new entrants come from countries with higher fertility than America's, not all do.

Filipinos, Vietnamese, and Indians show decreasing fertility upon settling in the United States. Incomers from these countries are also, on average, the best educated among those currently immigrating to the United States.

For the other national groups, planting roots in America increases their fertility rate. Most immigrants originate in countries that have economically, socially, or politically unfavorable conditions. Not only does that discourage child bearing, but it also curtails education. As a consequence, they arrive much less schooled than Filipinos, Vietnamese, and Indians but much more willing to bear children. Education versus fertility.

We don't want immigrants?

9

Which Ones, Then?

Throughout this book I have aimed to refute the apprehensions of opponents of further immigration. The evidence in Chapters 2 through 7 undermines arguments against *legal* immigrants. It shows instead how uniformly they benefit us.

By partaking in our society, immigrants affirm their faith in our system and in the very idea of America. They strengthen our education, bolstering our global competitiveness. They nurture our inventiveness and our innovation instincts. They invigorate our economy and balance our demographic prospects. They add to our civic vitality and gradually regenerate our elites. Their children bring us diversity and often modernity and sophistication. Their cumulative contributions help us adapt to the demands of a rapidly changing modern world.

❖ ❖ ❖

In *That Used to Be Us,* Thomas Friedman and Michael Mandelbaum reflect about America's potential and its magic:

"We have greater potential than any other country to thrive in the future by becoming the world's most attractive launching pad—the place where everyone wants to come to work, invent, collaborate, or start something new in order to get the most out of the new hyper-connected world."[1]

…and…

"If we want to keep [America's] magic, we need immigration reform that guarantees that we will always attract and retain in a legal, orderly fashion, the world first-round aspirational and intellectual draft choices."[2]

In the same vein, Singapore's elder statesman Lee Kwan Yew thought in 2010:

"China can draw on a talent pool of 1.3 billion people; the United States can draw on a talent pool of seven billion people."

From Singapore, he sees that we continue to exercise a most powerful draw on much of the world. So should we open the immigration doors to 6.69 billion to add to our current three hundred and ten million and let them all come in? If not all, which ones? How many?

Fashioning Immigration Policy

Today's desirable immigrant is not the immigrant of yore. Once Emma Lazarus wrote, "Give me your poor, your tired, your huddled masses, yearning to breathe free." Now her verses might proclaim

"Give me your aspiring and enterprising, your risk-takers and innovators, your dreamers of the possible dream."

Thus recast, her verses can inspire a new immigration policy for the United States—a policy designed from clear-sighted strength, not from doubt, defensiveness, or hesitation; a policy that can persuade and enlist all concerned. It must gain national consensus and convince doubters and opponents that virtually nothing but benefits stream from qualified, legal immigrants. It also needs to take into account the views of advocates of open borders, partisans—in effect, of Emma Lazarus' original verses.

Some principles. To serve America's long-term interests, certain principles must brace our immigration policy.

Principle: keep the US energized, adaptable, and generating change

This principle argues for a diversified immigrant workforce: of the highly trained, especially in science and technology; of the skilled, though not necessarily much educated; of the less educated but hard working. It also invites the entrepreneurial and the risk-assuming.

Principle: strengthen our civic vitality

This principle invites newcomers receptive to our culture and to our institutions, those potentially willing to commit to us by becoming engaged citizens. Our government needs to encourage this process by providing for the assimilation of newcomers to our cultural expectations.

Principle: establish upper boundaries for a balanced population growth

Our interest demands limits to further demographic growth but also to balance the population toward a steady replacement rate. This calls for youthful and fertile immigrants. It also necessitates establishing upper limits to the number of yearly entrants, with clearly specified standards for admission.

These principles define criteria for whom we should want and whom we shouldn't.

Whom We Want

As a general criterion, we need to favor the ambitious, the hardworking, those willing to improve themselves—hard as such traits may be to determine beforehand. We need to seek these fundamental qualities in desirable immigrants in the hope that they will embrace America, become citizens, and raise a productive second generation.

Equally indispensable, we should require new immigrants to come legally by applying for a visa. This step ensures a modicum of exposure to our legal and constitutional culture and to the spirit of our institutions. It also filters out those unwilling or unable to take part in our civic life. Most immigrants perceive America's access to opportunity, but not all of them know that it depends on the rule of the law.

Beyond these general considerations, we want to attract specific categories of immigrants.

The well-educated. In preceding chapters we saw how educated immigrants benefit us across the board: in our education, in science, and in our economic, social, and cultural life. The educated are also likely to arrive with a clearer understanding of the United States, as I did. They are consequently more apt to commit to our civic ways.

When I applied for a permanent resident visa that would entitle me to a green card, the US consulate in Buenos Aires tested me for elementary knowledge of the American constitutional system. After I was able to submit an affidavit by an American citizen regarding my putative reliability, the United States granted me a visa. I arrived in 1960 with higher education and some understanding of what the United States expected of me—not only of what to expect of the United States. Despite not initially grasping the details of this new country, it took me only weeks to absorb the idea of America and to commit mind and spirit to becoming American.

A note on "Hispanics," generally suspected of contributing little at advanced levels. They have, in fact, added great numbers of professionals to American society. The Pew Hispanic Center for 2009 lists millions (the figures between parentheses indicate foreign-born): 1,241,000 (508,000) managers; 288,000 (97,000) financial executives; 217,000 (69,000) computer scientists and mathematicians; 195,000 (77,000) architects and engineers; 95,000 (35,000) various scientists; 131,000 (33,000) lawyers; 851,000 (263,000) educators; and 527,000 (163,000) doctors, nurses, and medical technicians.

We can employ unlimited numbers of the educated—demand far exceeds domestic supply. As a bonus, they also reproduce close to a replacement rate: mostly two children per couple.

The skilled. At this writing, the rapidly automating and robotizing US economy suffers an unemployment rate in the 8 percent range (probably even greater if we count the discouraged). Yet skilled jobs go begging: air conditioning and heating, welding, nutritionists, nursing aides, nuclear technicians, or generalized mechanics, not to mention those able to monitor computation-based instruments. We have unemployability rather than mere unemployment because we don't produce nearly enough natives with mechanical and reasonable computational skills. To satisfy our evolving needs, we must attract newcomers, even those with an often limited but specialized education. In an article on a renascent American auto industry, *Time* (Dec. 19, 2011) illustrates the nature of the skills we require:

> Fiat sent over [to Chrysler, in Detroit] some two dozen workers from its Pomigliano plant in southern Italy to teach its World Class Manufacturing program. Rather than bringing in squads of industrial engineers to dictate the exact sequence of each assembly process, workers

were trained to use analytical tools to help them *understand each process* [my italics] in the 400 or so workstations on the floor.

We have an acute shortage of nurses, as our population grows older and its health deteriorates. In 2010 demand existed for 2.34 million nurses, but supply stood at only 2.07 million, a deficit of 12 percent; among emergency and acute care nurses the deficit stood at 17 percent. But Philippine nurses potentially to the rescue. Highly-trained and certified as registered nurses, they staff our hospitals across the land, partly reducing our deficit. Rosario is one such highly skilled Philippine nurse:

> I immigrated to the United States five years ago and found immediately a professional position in a quality American hospital. Previously I held similar positions for brief periods in the United Arab Emirates and in Britain. I came to America because it appeals to me culturally and because of opportunity to earn better pay. My overriding priority in emigrating was to repay my parents for the sacrifices they made in providing me with an education. I will become, enthusiastically, an American citizen as soon as the law allows.

As of September 2009, our government allotted 2,800 working visas a year for Philippine nurses—while 56,896 are waiting to immigrate and work in the United States.[3]

The less, or even little educated. Immigrants with less education fill needs that will not vanish, either in our economy or in our society. A dynamic economy creates prosperity, which generates many jobs that require little education. The Bureau of Labor Statistics projects that for the period 2002–2012 the economy will generate five million jobs requiring only short-term on the job training. This figure applies to only the top fourteen job categories. The 2008 recession may have affected the actual numbers, but clearly, in addition to those top fourteen categories, the economy will create many more millions of such jobs.[4] This work pays low wages and many natives refuse it (see "They Take Our Jobs!" in Chapter 5).

Immigrants, currently mostly of the illegal variety, take these jobs willingly. We want lawful immigrants to take them henceforth. This is delicate. Among the less educated, some demonstrate great willingness to improve themselves educationally and otherwise (think of the Haitians in Chapter 7), while others exhibit aversion to education, as we see in Chapter 3. But they also bring needed demographic fertility.

This calls for a special comment about less educated Mexicans. They constitute the majority of our current illegals, *but if they come lawfully, we should want them.* They work hard—a self-evident proposition; they are honest (see Table 8.1); and they are young. Prejudice will not serve us well.

The "inter-migrants." In the twenty-first century the world has shrunk in time and space. Traveling forth *and back* has become easy and cheap. This has generated a new type: the "inter-migrants." They don't fit the traditional category of "immigrant" committed more or less permanently to a new country. Generally well-educated and well-qualified, inter-migrants are typically dissatisfied with their home country and disposed to emigrate. They have options and choices. They may prefer one country to another. They may intend their stay in the new country for a specific duration, to eventually return home in an enhanced position.

I came to the United States because I was offered a good job in a new industry that I found exciting. My other emigration choices had been Canada and the United Kingdom. I don't think that in either I would have achieved the same level of success. Here, there are opportunities that don't exist in other countries. Living in the United States had several consequences. Because I felt discriminated against on account of my race, I withdrew socially, but on the other hand, wanting to prove myself, it stimulated me to exceed my goals. This strengthened my self-respect. I have also reinvented myself several times, because in America that is possible. Had I immigrated to the United Kingdom or Canada, probably none of this would have happened. Yet I am still considering retiring to another country where blacks are not discriminated against.

—*James, the Jamaican scientist and researcher with an American PhD in electrical engineering*

We should regard such inter-migrants receptively. If genuinely useful to our society, their presence, even of limited duration, can benefit us. They may also stay for good or even become citizens while retaining a base at home. Rosario, the Philippine nurse above, comes to mind. After all, America can seduce: our law-based society, our open markets, our liberal democracy, our informality, our excellent universities that may not obtain in their countries become the very reasons they want to emigrate.

The foreign students. They contribute powerfully to our economy. As we saw in Chapter 3, in the academic year 2007–2008, six hundred and twenty-three thousand foreign students spent $15.4 billion here.[5] The largest international group, one hundred and fifty-seven thousand students in 2010–2011, came from China. At the University of California, Davis, some five thousand international students from fifty-six countries enrolled in 2009–2010, constituting 15 percent of the student body.

Most importantly, these foreign students may stay or return to energize us through their generally fine education and often through their enterprising spirit. Several of my interviewees fit both the student and the inter-migrant model. They came to study but stayed or returned to the United States. Most became citizens. Among them:

Miguel, from Costa Rica, who just wanted an American education and then return to Costa Rica. He earned a master's degree in electrical engineering, stayed, and founded a high-tech enterprise with headquarters in both Silicon Valley and Santiago de Chile.

Or *Ariel*, from Argentina, who earned an MBA from MIT, went back to Argentina, but returned to the United States specifically to found a high-tech enterprise, which he did.

Or *Maria Luisa*, from Colombia, who came for a secondary education. She then went back to Colombia but found that she couldn't function there as a professional woman. She returned to the United States and earned a PhD. Along the way she met love, married an American, and stayed. She teaches and has two American-born, sophisticated sons.

Or *Ahmed*, from Pakistan, who came to study engineering. He didn't intend to immigrate and wanted to return to Pakistan upon completion of his studies, but he too met love and got married. Now an American, he has contributed decades of engineering expertise to the United States.

Or *Anand* from India, who came to Illinois to study architecture and planned to return to India. He stayed, founded an architecture firm in California, became a citizen. He travels to India regularly, but considers the US his home.

California's Silicon Valley thrives with multiple foreign-born graduates from Stanford University, the University of California, MIT, and many other leading American schools. But our "war on terror" politics reject many. Speaking specifically of South Koreans, *The Economist* (Dec. 17, 2011) says:

> Some 13 percent of Korean tertiary students study abroad…In recent years, many have come home, not least because the American government, in a fit of self-destructive foolishness, made it much harder after Sept. 11, 2011, for foreign students to work in America after they graduate. A survey by Vivek Wadhwa, of Duke University, found that

most foreign students at American universities feared they would not be able to obtain a work visa. And since the application process is long and humiliating, many do not even bother to try. America's loss is Korea's (and India's and China's) gain.

California Representative Zoe Lofgren has sponsored the IDEA Act to remedy this problem. It allows students earning advanced degrees in the United States to remain after they complete their studies. She says:

> It makes no sense for us to educate the world's brightest students and then ship them back to their home countries to compete against us. My bill would allow some of the world's sharpest minds to stay in the United States and help us grow our economy.

The IDEA Act faces a rocky road in Congress.

Whom We Don't Want

Broadly speaking, we don't want those who don't fit the preceding criteria. Certainly we don't welcome common-criminal ex-denizens of foreign jails, or alumni of Al Qaeda terrorist training camps, or the few who come with the expectation to freeload. Beyond such self-evident categories, we should either not desire or consider ambivalently some others.

The huddled masses. We can't afford them any longer—not demographically, nor economically, politically, or socially. Circumstances have changed since the late nineteenth century, the time of Lazarus' poem. Back then there were some seventy million people in the United States, if that. The land was rather empty and we had great need for manual labor. Meanwhile, the country has filled out and we have automated the economy.

In order to function, our society requires much higher education, skills, and general levels of knowledge than those of Lazarus' day. Moreover, we already have large numbers of the huddled, many of which entered illegally in recent years. Our population will grow organically and through controlled immigration anyway, but can we afford a population boom?

We must also examine the moral case. My friend Bob, grandson of immigrants himself, challenges me:

> Wanting only the educated and filtered types is elitism. What about the "huddled masses yearning to be free"?...Are we getting that selfish, to want/allow in only those we absolutely know will contribute mightily to get ahead and make good on their hard-won education? We treat people equally here. Some will be just getting their first chance at a real education. What's your stand on that?

I can agree with Bob's generous sentiment. We should indeed remember that we are a moral nation and that generations of huddled masses have proven themselves. We should nevertheless not assume that in Emma Lazarus' day we admitted the huddled out of humanitarian considerations. We did it because we needed them to fill the land and provide cheap labor. We must not still our humanitarian impulses but reserve them for those fleeing for their lives from tyrannies. The romantic view of the United States as the last refuge of the oppressed masses, yearning to breathe free, was never our policy, nor can it become it now.

Those coming illegally. Let's be clear about the reason for opposing them: they cross our borders because, consciously or not, they escape societies in which the law neither serves nor defends them. They come to the United States because our laws will protect them, whether they understand that or not. Being largely uneducated, they mostly don't know that the law is the foundation stone of our national community. Lacking exposure to the sources of our social compact, they become less than promising members of our society. Many resist learning English, [6] the language and the culture in which our system is conceived. Many don't improve themselves educationally (see next); often they send their children to bilingual schools, where not much English is spoken or learned. This latter assertion stems from personal experience, because I tutor at such a school.

Those who don't desire to improve themselves. The Pew Hispanic Center provides dismal data. For 2009, it indicates that only 9.7 percent of "Latinos" graduate from college (compared with 49.9 percent of "Asians") and that 20.4 percent drop out of high school (compared with 2 percent of Asians). The Pew Center doesn't indicate how many of these Latinos belong to the first generation of actual immigrants, nor whether they came lawfully. A generous American policy cannot tar entire ethnicities with the same brush, but the Pew Center data require a sober assessment of how we should select immigrants.

We need to consider warily those unwilling to commit to us. In Chapter 6, we saw that 57 percent of immigrants don't choose to become citizens. Of those who do, only slightly more than half seem to vote, largely the more educated or assimilated. Among such new citizens, these behaviors seem to transfer to the second generation. By not voting, they don't commit to our civic expectations. Should we consider them with some ambivalence? After all, many contribute to the economy and to education. If there is a practical limit to how many immigrants we can admit, should these be among them?

Finally, a sacred cow. We need to question our current policy of granting preferential, practically open-border access to families of immigrants. In addition to spouses and minor children of US citizens, how many members of their extended family and to what degree of relation should we admit? We need to also ask what they will contribute. If this policy responds broadly to a humanitarian impulse, it still requires judgment about how many such family members deserve no-questions-asked admittance.

Having listed all these undesirable categories, I wouldn't be too fanatical about enforcing the selectivity I advocate. There is no way to keep out those truly determined to enter. Who knows what talent may come on the coattails of determination.

The Immigrants' View

In proposing a reformed US immigration policy, I offer the personal opinion of a naturalized American. My recommendations also largely concur with the views of many new citizens whom I interviewed. I asked them, "Should we encourage immigration?" Their responses range from strong support, to caution, to skepticism, as in the following, short sampler.

Most strongly support further immigration:

Yes, we should encourage legal immigration, but there is little point in trying to select desirable immigrants. This is a massive, uncontrollable force and immigrants will sort themselves out once they settle. We should encourage them to come and stay. They will tilt the system in a positive direction.

—*entrepreneur from Costa Rica*

Yes, we should encourage it strongly because immigrants add $3 to the economy for every dollar they cost. They add education, cultural experiences, and diversity. They beget evolutionary results in a Darwinian sense.

—*graduate student from Mexico*

Of course we should encourage immigration. As to what kind, that regulates itself. Immigration has always been an elemental force, and policy can only fine-tune it. Immigrants are of course enormously helpful to this country.

—*engineer from Greece*

Certainly. Closed societies have not progressed because they fence themselves off from innovation in all respects.

—*engineer from France*

Yes, we should. Immigration is nothing but positive. Closed borders are neither natural nor in the modern spirit. Opposition to immigration is a thing of the past.

—*entrepreneur from Argentina*

We should. Silicon Valley runs because of immigrants. But we should welcome not only the educated. We should show some compassion for all those who need our opportunities.

—*high-tech executive from Italy*

Yes, we should encourage more legal immigration. We should allow everyone in, regardless of qualifications, because you never know into what kind of person an immigrant will bloom in this country. Also, immigrants are agents of innovation by their very nature and we need that. Of course, certain qualities are desirable, such as drive and intelligence.

—*computer programmer from England*

…and many more. But some voice caution:

Yes, America should encourage immigration, but selectively. Encourage good people to come, then provide them with the means to stay legally. Ship law breakers back to Mexico.

—*nurse from Mexico*

Yes, but cautiously. We should accept only immigrants with affidavits vouching for their honesty and good character.

—*beautician from Russia*

Yes, but cautiously. Need controls. Bring in those willing to work, even if poor. The criterion should be: do they have skills, not family. Also, will they integrate? I counsel Mexican immigrants, probably illegal, and they don't integrate—in fact, make no effort to integrate. Not desirable.

—*teacher from Colombia*

A few express downright skepticism:

Perhaps. I don't feel strongly about it, but if we are to admit immigrants, they should be young and willing to work. We should not admit some of those old people who just use benefits that arise from our hard work.

—*small business owner from Iran*

I am conflicted about that. When a highly-trained or skilled person immigrates to the United States, his home country loses his talents. America's gain is another country's loss. Consider all the nurses that are leaving Africa, where they are so needed. Also, many youthful gangs that threaten our security seem composed of immigrants.

—*engineer from Colombia*

Brass Tacks

Much talk about reforming immigration policy currently agitates politicians in and out of Congress. It concerns almost exclusively the fixing of a past burdened by illegal immigrants. But a reformed immigration policy needs to address the future instead, calibrated to our existing and developing needs: economic, educational, and demographic. It should prioritize the following components:

Selectivity. Our domestic interest precludes open borders and compels us to admit immigrants selectively. A new policy must allow *and encourage* a broad variety of immigrants:

- the educated and the highly trained, especially in science and technology
- the skilled, though not necessarily much educated
- the less educated, but hard working.

All, of course, need sifting for good character, as well as willingness to work and to become contributing citizens. Implicitly, this policy excludes individuals attempting to enter the country by bypassing our legal requirements or those intending to game our system.

Demographic factors. More than any other consideration, the size of our existing and inevitably growing population reinforces the need for selectivity. To balance our population toward a steady replacement rate, we must invite youthful and fertile immigrants. This aspect of selectivity also challenges our tradition of accepting extended families of US citizens in practically limitless numbers. Demography thus requires that we legislate explicit criteria for the number of immigrants admitted yearly.

Assimilation and integration. We saw in Chapter 6 that not all new migrants assimilate and even fewer integrate as civically contributing citizens. Traditionally, assimilation to US linguistic and cultural norms proceeded organically. Some adapted readily and quickly, others not at all, and most fell somewhere in the middle. Today that natural process receives some aid. Major corporations like Wal-Mart, UPS, Northrop-Grumman, Western Union, and Marriot International have undertaken initiatives to teach English to their foreign-born employees. So do several dozen other major businesses, as do some smaller companies.

Learning English is, however, only one step in assimilation. The concern for many native-born who oppose further immigration centers on integration—the willingness to participate fully in our civic life. A new immigration policy cannot side-step this political reality. To further integration, the new policy should include active provisions aimed mostly at the less educated newcomers. A possible model for such legislation currently circulates through

Congress. Introduced by Representative Mike Honda, the Strengthen and Unite Communities through Civics Education and English Development (SUCCEED) Act provides immigrant families access to critical assistance such as English language and civics education. The SUCCEED Act intends to "help immigrant communities integrate into the American fabric and maximize their social and economic contributions."

Humanitarian considerations. A humanitarian consciousness forms part of our national temper. An immigration policy must include specific criteria to reflect this concern.

Provision for nonimmigrants. Numerous well-educated, highly trained foreign-born, often with an entrepreneurial, risk-taking bent, wish to enter the United States. They may not desire permanent residence or qualify as immigrants. Their work can benefit our economy, however, sometimes in critical areas. Our national interest strongly recommends that we welcome them. In this regard, H-IB and EB-I and EB-2 visas, which begin with a temporary green card, should receive priority attention. We should build into these visas the possibility (encouragement?) for eventual permanent residence and naturalization.

Frequent review and updating. In an accelerating and rapidly changing world, nothing remains static. Nor can our immigration policy. It needs to flex with changing circumstances. We cannot allow it to age and become irrelevant to our social, economic, and demographic realities. In formulating it, we must build in a mechanism of frequent (yearly?) reviews of all its provisions.

Implementation. A new policy must specify measures for its competent implementation, as considered in the Appendix below.

Bear Their Voices

You have now heard the voices of immigrants from thirty-seven different countries (and of some of their offspring). They have animated my narrative and framed its tone. You have read about their confidence in the United States and, most often, their commitment to it. They expressed almost unanimous optimism about America and often a desire to build a new American identity for themselves. When I asked them whether the United States was in decline, most dismissed that notion (the few who believed it was thought the decline only temporary).

Echoing their voices, my concluding plea to doubting natives:

> Allow us immigrants to continue building this great country with the optimism and the can-do spirit of your ancestors. Let's together forge a new immigration policy guided by the voices in this book!

Appendix - Implementing an Immigration Policy

The effectiveness of a new immigration policy will depend on the United States State Department's management of a smart visa system and on judicious decisions by competent consular officers at home and abroad.

Visas. A sound visa system pursues several objectives. It optimizes the potential contributions of the migrants and minimizes the negative. It attracts particularly desirable types of newcomers who possess characteristics that meet our national needs. Such a system requires a thoughtful spectrum of visas—for immigrants, of course, but also various other kinds. It must include a variety of temporary visas, principally for those who wish to do work we need. Any category of temporary visas should include provisions for possible subsequent permanent residence and eventual naturalization.

Of particular importance are H-1B visas, to which I refer above and in Chapter 5 ("Red Herrings") and which apply to specified occupations in fields requiring highly specialized knowledge. (As of this writing, Senator Grassley, of Iowa, is blocking the pertinent legislation out of concern for the employment and earnings on Americans.) Equally important are initial visas for foreign students and subsequent provisions for those among them who desire to stay and work in the United States.

FLASH! On May 22, 2012, the Senate has introduced a bipartisan immigration bill to create two new types of visa to attract and keep immigrants skilled in science, technology, engineering and mathematics. Called Start-Up Act 2.0, it responds to industry pressure and applies to foreign students who receive graduate degrees in the US. It also creates a new visa for 75,000 skilled immigrants who start a new business in the US, employ Americans and invest or raise capital in the United States. This bill faces an uncertain future in the House.

Our consular staffs. An intelligent visa system requires a deft and, redundant to say, diplomatic management. Much will depend on our consular personnel—its understanding of the spirit of the new legislation and its attitudes toward visa applicants. Indeed, the State Department bureaucracy can cause damage to the nation's interests. Refer to the above quote from *The Economist*: "since the application process is long and humiliating, many do not even bother to try." We do want them to try and, if qualified, to succeed. We don't need to make it an obstacle course administered by the obtuse.

Concern about indifferent bureaucratic behavior extends to our missions abroad. A new immigration policy will succeed only if our consulates implement it aptly. Most Americans have little awareness of our consulates. They protect our interests when we travel, but their most consequential effect is on foreigners. Skilled interviewing by competent consular officers during the application process allows us to select desirable individuals of presumably good character and with the potential to become contributing members of our society.

Tough assignments for the staffs of our consulates: how to determine ambition, enterprising spirit, and the ability to blossom in America. A visa interview can go a long way toward determining whether an individual has the potential for commitment or merely expects to coast along in America.

As we saw in Chapter 6, some immigrant groups tend to take to American citizenship more readily. This necessitates cultural awareness by our consular staffs.

In 2011 *Immigration Daily*, "the news source for legal professionals," stated that the majority of our consular officers conduct themselves professionally and treat visa applicants with respect. But far from all:

> In the last six months [of 2009] alone, our clients have dealt with an openly rude and hostile consular section chief in Surabaya; a consul general in Jakarta unfamiliar with the requirement of disclosing factual reasons for a visa refusal; a consular chief in Yerevan asking an applicant why he retained a lawyer; and the post in Moscow issuing visas with less than maximum validity, impermissibly readjudicating an approved petition, and seeking to require a principal visa holder to return to Moscow before issuing visas to his dependents, in violation of the Foreign Affairs Manual.

> Unfortunately, these consular issues are not atypical. In fact, over the course of our twenty years in handling consular matters, these problems are common: a screaming consular officer in Tashkent who would call security if an applicant questioned her decision; an officer in Warsaw who would not allow an applicant to use an interpreter and wrongfully accused him of a sham marriage (the shocked applicant had a stroke the following day and died); the post in Lagos sitting on an IV application for three years; an arrogant officer in Moscow who frequently called applicants 'liars' and was profiled in a Russian newspaper for her abusive and condescending treatment of applicants.

In personal conversations, foreigners have told me that they decided not to apply for an American visa and chose another country because our consular representatives are so rude; also because the bureaucratic requirements take infinite time. Skilled and sensitive consular officers form America's front line. They can project our soft power. The State Department needs to hire and train them in accordance to their importance to our national interest.

We do want immigrants

Notes

Chapter 1: We Need Immigrants

1. Thomas Friedman and Michael Mandelbaum, *That Used to Be Us* (:Farrar, Straus and Giroux, 2011), 137.
2. For detailed data, see www.pollingreport.com/immigration.htm.
3. Federation for American Immigration Reform, *Why America Needs an Immigration Time-Out*, www.fairus.org/site/PageServer?pagename=iic.
4. Southern Poverty Law Center, *Intelligence Report Winter 2008*, Issue Number 132.
5. The site pajamasmedia.com/.../lets-face-it-many-americans-oppose-all-immigration provides rich details.
6. Peter Schrag, *Not Fit for Our Society* (: University of California Press, 2010), 241.
7. See boston.com, May 30, 2009.
8. Friedman and Mandelbaum, *That Used To Be Us*, 17.

Chapter 2: Affirming Faith in America

1. Donald Worster, *A River Running West: The Life of John Wesley Powell* (New York: Oxford University Press, 2002), 384.

Chapter 3: Strengthening Education

1. Reported in www.quickanded.com/2010/12/u-s-college-gradu-ation-rate-stays-pretty-much-exactly-the-same.html, December 2, 2010.

2. *New York Times*, "Putting Our Brains on Hold," August 7, 2010.

3. National Science Foundation, *2002 INDICATORS—Science and Engineering*, nsf.gov/statistics/seind02/c2/c2s2.htm.

4. The Pew Hispanic Center's report, *Statistical Portrait of Hispanics in the United States* (2009) Table 22.

5. Reported by John Baumgartner and Lynn Schoch, Indiana University Office of International Services.

6. Ample information on immigrant entrepreneurs appears in David Card, *Is the New Immigration Really So Bad?*, National Bureau of Economic Research, 2005; also study report, *America's New Immigrant Entrepreneurs*, Duke University Master of Engineering Management Program, January 4, 2007; also School of Information, UC Berkeley, people.ischool.berkeley.edu/.../Americas_new_immigrant_entre-prene; and the Marion Ewing Kauffman Foundation, 2007.

7. *New York Times*, June, 5, 2005.

8. Much pertinent information appears in various sources. Patricia Fernandez-Kelly and Alejandro Portes, eds., *Exceptional Outcomes: Achievement in Education and Employment Among Children of Immigrants* (Thousand Oaks: Sage Publications,), 138 ff.

9. See also op. cit., *Exceptional Outcomes*, 186 ff.

10. Hans Johnson, *Immigrants and Education*, www.ppic.org/content/pubs/jtf/JTF_ImmigrantsEducationJTF.pdf. The site documents levels of different immigrants' education. It also demonstrates strong educational progress across generations.

11. Op. cit., Card, *Is the New Immigration Really So Bad?*

12. Op. cit., Friedman and Mandelbaum, *That Used To Be Us*, 41.

13. *National Science Foundation*, www.nsf.gov/statistics/nsf03312/c3/c3s2.htm.

14. *The Economist*, "The Future of Jobs," September 10–16, 2011.

15. Richard T. Herman and Robert L. Smith, *Immigrant, Inc.* (New York: John Wiley and Sons, 2010), XXVI.

16. See website www.pomeradonews.com/.../are-foreign-grad-students-good-for-america.

17. Merage Foundation for the American Dream, American Dream Fellow, 2010, http://www.meragefoundations.com/mfad_fellows2010.html.

Chapter 4: Nurturing Innovation and Inventiveness

1. *The Atlantic Century*, "Benchmarking EU & US Innovation and Competitiveness," February 2009.

2. Op. cit., Duke University Master of Engineering Management Program, January 4, 2007.

3. School of Information, UC Berkeley, people.ischool.berkeley.edu/.../Americas_new_immigrant_entreprene.

4. Op. cit., Herman and Smith, *Immigrant, Inc.*, XXIV.

Chapter 5: Spurring the Economy

1. Op. cit. Herman and Smith, *Immigrant, Inc.*, Exhibit A.7 and http://www.futureofcapitalism.com/688/immigrant-inc.

2. Marion Ewing Kauffman Foundation, *Index of Entrepreneurial Activity*, the study report *America's New Immigrant Entrepreneurs*.

3. Op. cit. Kauffman Foundation, *Index of Entrepreneurial Activity*, May 23, 2006.

4. Interview with 2010 OppenheimerFunds/NFTE National Youth Entrepreneurship Challenge finalists Belma Ahmetovic and Zermina Velic; see also *2010 Network for Teaching Entrepreneurship,* www.nfte. com .

5. Robert Fairlie, *Race and Entrepreneurial Success,* (Cambridge: MIT Press, 2007).

6. Julian Simon, Cato Institute, *Cato Policy Report,* September/October 1995.

7. National Research Council, *The New Americans,* 1997, 235. An exhaustive report on the effects of immigration on American life. See also *Bloomberg View* editors, June 9, 2011.

8. Op. cit. Kauffman Foundation, *Index of Entrepreneurial Activity,* May 23, 2006.

9. Giovanni Peri, *The Effect of Immigrants on US Employment and Productivity,* August 30, 2010, FRBSF, Economic Letter.

10. *Economist's View,* "David Card on Immigration and US Cities," economistsview.typepad.com/economistsview/.../david-card-on-i.htm. Cached Similar

11. "Immigrants Benefit American Workers," March 2, 2006, news. ucdavis.edu/search/news_detail.lasso?id=7622.

12. Nell Henderson, *Washington Post,* April 15, 2006.

13. Mark Whitehouse, "Some Firms Struggle to Hire Despite High Unemployment," *Wall Street Journal,* August 9, 2010.

14. See *BrightFutureJobs.com* www.h1b.info, a lobby strongly opposed to granting H-1B visas.

Chapter 6: Becoming American

1. US Census Bureau, *2009 American Community Survey.*

2. Leon Bouvier, *Embracing America—A Look at which Immigrants Become Citizens* (Center for Immigration Studies, July 1996).

3. See usgovinfo.about.com/od/thepoliticalsystem/a/whynotvote.htm for the California Voter Foundation results of a statewide survey on the attitudes of infrequent voters and citizens eligible to vote but not registered.

4. US Census Bureau, *Voting and Registration in the Election of November 2008—Detailed Tables.*

5. *Los Angeles Times,* "Drop in Young Voter Registration Bodes Badly for Obama," December 30, 2011.

6. Adapted from Brown et al., *Immigrants and Substance Use: Findings from the 1999–2001 National Survey on Drug Use and Health,* http://oas. samhsa.gov/immigrants/immigrants.htm#tabc8 (06/26/06) and "Alcohol and Drug Abuse by Natives vs. Immigrants," http://cac. hhd.org/pdf/FAQ2_RWJ.pdf.

Chapter 7: The Second Generation

1. Julian L. Simon, Cato Institute, *IMMIGRATION: The Demographic and Economic Facts,* December 11, 1995). Also Julian L. Simon, *The Economic Consequences of Immigration* (: The University of Michigan Press, 1989).

2. Op. cit., *Exceptional Outcomes,* 12 ff., *No Margin for Error.*

3. Op. cit., *Exceptional Outcomes,* 90 ff., *Disparities in Educational Success of Immigrants.*

4. US Department of Education, National Center for Education Statistics. *The Condition of Education 2011* (NCES 2011-033), Indicator 20.

5. National Research Council, The General Social Survey, 1997, cited in *Intergenerational Educational Mobility, The New Americans,* Appendix 7.A, 355.

6. Op. cit. *Exceptional Outcomes,* cited in *"Here's Your Diploma, Mom!" Family Obligation and Multiple Pathways to Success,* 237 ff.

7. See Wikipedia, en.wikipedia.org/wiki/Salman_Khan_ (educator).

8. *Newsweek,* July 19, 2010, 50.

9. The Pew Hispanic Center provides a detailed discussion of the subject in its report *Hispanics, High School Dropouts and the GED,* May 13, 2010.

10. Table 8.1 and related information in this section stem from reports from the Migration Policy Institute, *Migration Information Source,* particularly from reports of June 2008 and October 2010.

11. Rob Paral and Associates, *Benchmarks of Immigrant Civic Engagement,* July 2010.

Chapter 8: Balancing Our Population Growth

1. Public Policy Institute of California, *How Fertility Changes Across Immigrant Generations,* April 2002, Issue 58.

2. Northeastern University's Center for Labor Market Studies, Nell Henderson, "How Immigration Spurs the Economy," *Washington Post,* April 15, 2006.

3. Centers for Disease Control, *Births: Preliminary Data for 2002.*

4. Population Reference Bureau, *2010 Fertility Rate 2.0;* also from 2010 World Population Data Sheet, July 28, 2010.

5. Center for Immigration Studies, *Immigration and Rising US Fertility,* February 2012.

6. CIA, *The World Factbook,* Country Comparison: Total Fertility Rate, 2009.

7. CIA, *The World Factbook,* October 24, 2011.

Chapter 9: Which Ones Then?

1. Op. cit. Friedman and Mandelbaum, *That Used to Be Us,* 354.

2. Op. cit. Friedman and Mandelbaum, *That Used to Be Us,* 226.

3. *Nursing Shortage*, Wikipedia, December 2011.

4. *Monthly Labor Review*, February 2004, Table 4, 101.

5. John Baumgartner and Lynn Schoch, Indiana University Office of International Services.

6. Nearly 75 percent of Mexican immigrants in 2006 were limited-English proficient. Migration Policy Institute, *Mexican Immigrants in the United States*, April 2008.

Index

www.ingramcontent.com/pod-product-compliance
Lightning Source LLC
Chambersburg PA
CBHW070012300526
45794CB00001B/291